Food and Nutrition

VOLUME 1

Acid Indigestion *to* Calcium

EDITORIAL ADVISERS

Dayle Hayes

Rachel Laudan

Marshall Cavendish
99 White Plains Road
Tarrytown, New York 10591-9001

www.marshallcavendish.com

©2009 Marshall Cavendish Corporation

Library of Congress Cataloging-in-Publication Data

Food and nutrition / editorial advisers, Dayle Hayes, Rachel Laudan.
     v. cm.
Contents: v. 1. Acid indigestion to calcium—v. 2. Calories to energy drinks—v. 3. Enzymes to German cuisine—v. 4 Glycemic index to legislation and food—v. 5 Legumes to pellagra—v. 6 Pesticides to South American cuisines—v. 7 South Asian cuisines to yogurt—v. 8 Indexes.

ISBN 978-0-7614-7817-1 (set: alk. paper)—ISBN 978-0-7614-7820-1 (v.: alk. paper)—ISBN 978-0-7614-7821-8 (v. 2: alk. paper)—ISBN 978-0-7614-7822-5 (v. 3: alk. paper)—ISBN 978-0-7614-7824-9 (v.4: alk. paper)—ISBN 978-0-7614-7825-6 (v. 5: alk. paper)—ISBN 978-0-7614-7826-3 (v. 6: alk. paper)—ISBN 978-0-7614-7827-0 (v. 7: alk. paper)—ISBN 978-0-7614-7828-7 (v. 8: alk. paper)
1. Food—Encyclopedias. 2. Nutrition—Encyclopedias. I. Hayes, Dayle. II. Laudan, Rachel, 1944-

TX349.F572 2009
641.303--dc22

             2008062301

Printed in Malaysia

12 11 10 09 08 1 2 3 4 5

Dayle Hayes is a consultant, author, and educator, and currently serves as president of Nutrition for the Future, Inc. An American Dietetic Association award winner, she also is a media spokeswoman and past president of the Montana Dietetic Association.

Rachel Laudan trained as a historian of science and is a former professor of biology at the University of Hawaii. She is now an independent writer on the subject of food history and has received the Julia Child and the Sophie Coe awards, the two major prizes in the field.

Contributors: Eugene Anderson; Mindy Hermann; Laura Lambert; Rachel Laudan; Sheila Lewis; Annie Lux; Katharine Norman; Paul Schellinger; Mary Sisson; Densie Webb; Gwendolyn Wells; Chris Woodford

MARSHALL CAVENDISH
Editor: Stephanie Driver
Publisher: Paul Bernabeo
Production Manager: Michael Esposito

MTM PUBLISHING
President: Valerie Tomaselli
Executive Editor: Hilary W. Poole
Associate Editor: Tim Anderson
Editorial Coordinator: Zachary Gajewski
Editorial Assistant: Ingrid Wenzler
Illustrator: Richard Garratt
Copyeditor: Peter Jaskowiak
Designer: Patrice Sheridan
Indexer: AEIOU, Inc.

Alphabetical Table of Contents

VOLUME 3

VOLUME 4

VOLUME 5

VOLUME 6

Thematic Table of Contents

This thematic table of contents organizes the articles in this set into nine categories: cooking and eating; cuisines; cultural and social aspects of food; food safety; foods and drinks; foods and health; nutrition; production and business of food; weight and weight loss.

NUTRITION

FOODS AND HEALTH

Introduction

For young people in the twenty-first century, food choices can be complex and confusing, with their decisions complicated by mixed messages, advertising hype, and misinformation. In the modern world, food is everywhere, from vending machines at school to candy aisles at the convenience store, from cooking shows on TV to coffee shops on every corner, and from golden arches on the highway to super-size buckets of popcorn at the movies. Everywhere young people turn, there are snacks and drinks calling out to them with clever advertising slogans, brightly colored packages, and tantalizing aromas.

In the midst of all this food, there is also a heightened awareness about nutrition, weight control, and chronic diseases in childhood. News stories about the childhood obesity "epidemic" are widespread, and there have been numerous television shows focused specifically on the weight problems of young people. While adolescents are being pressured on one hand to "eat, eat, eat," they are simultaneously bombarded with unrealistic images of ultrathin, sculpted bodies in magazines, movies, and television shows. Nearly every celebrity, movie star, and model seems to have a diet or some easy way to melt the pounds away.

INCREASINGLY OVERWEIGHT

Although the media are fond of hyping an "obesity epidemic" among the young, many in the medical community do not apply the term *obesity* to young people. Nonetheless, those classified as overweight (the preferred term) among American children ages 6 to 11 more than doubled between 1980 and 2004, rising from 7 percent to 19 percent during that period. Likewise, the number of overweight adolescents (ages 12 to 19) more than tripled during the same period, increasing from 5 percent to 17 percent.

There is no single cause for the change in child and adolescent weights. Many factors have contributed to this trend, including more sedentary lifestyles, more screen entertainment (TVs and computers), the increasing size of food and beverage portions, the marketing of foods and beverages directly to young people, and greater access to snacks foods and soft drinks.

Overweight young people are at a higher risk for several health problems, including early onset of type 2 diabetes, elevated cholesterol levels, high blood pressure, asthma, and joint problems. According to the National Education Association, overweight youth report a lower quality of life, which can include harassment, discouragement, depression, and even discrimination at school. Overweight students also tend to have more school absences.

Pediatric experts agree that the best strategies for promoting a healthy weight, such as regular meals and daily physical activity, should involve the entire family. Restrictive diets are not recommended because they can compromise normal growth and lead to serious clinical eating disorders. Dieters are also more likely to engage in binge eating. Indeed, dieting may actually promote weight gain—a three-year survey of over 14,000 boys and girls showed that the dieters gained more weight than those who were not dieting.

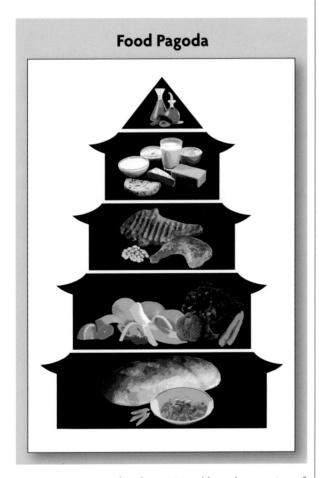

Food Pagoda

Many entries in *Food and Nutrition* address the question of what constitutes a healthy diet. The entry "Food Pyramid" explains how nutritionists worldwide have attempted to make healthy eating easier to visualize and understand with iconic representations such as this "food pagoda," which is used in China.

DIETING AND BODY IMAGE

While there is no doubt that excessive weight and weight gain are a major health concern for America's youth, it is important to look at the whole spectrum of weight-related issues when discussing young people and food. Young people grow up in a society obsessed with thinness, in an environment where dieting is the norm and a supplement industry vigorously promotes the use of potentially harmful products.

Many normal, and even some underweight, adolescents feel pressure to be thin. The attention focused on the obesity epidemic as well as the unrealistic images constantly seen in the media help to maintain this pressure. The 2005 Youth Risk Behavior Surveillance System (YRBSS), managed by the Centers for Disease Control and Prevention (CDC), reported that 31 percent of teenagers thought they were overweight and 46 percent were trying to lose weight. In this same sample, however, only 13 percent were actually overweight. (Overweight in young people is defined as having a body mass index that is higher than 95 percent of that of other people the same age.)

According to a 2006 study by the University of Minnesota's Project EAT (Eating among Teens), the use of diet pills by high-school-aged females nearly doubled over the five-year period from 1999 to 2004. Overall, the study found that 20 percent of the females surveyed had used diet pills by the age of 20. The study also discovered that teenage females who diet and follow unhealthful weight-control behaviors are at three times the risk of being overweight.

The combination of body dissatisfaction and risky dieting behaviors can lead to a serious, life-threatening disease for some young people. In the United States, an estimated 5 to 10 million adolescent girls and women, as well as 1 million boys and men, struggle with eating disorders and related conditions. Teachers, school counselors, and therapists report finding younger and younger children with disordered eating patterns and diagnosable eating disorders.

OVERFED BUT UNDERNOURISHED

Clearly, U.S. children are getting plenty of calories. It would be one thing if these calories came from nutrient-rich foods. Sadly, this is not the case. Whether they are overweight or not, young people in the United States are often poorly nourished in a land of plenty. Here are just a few of the statistics:

- Although average intakes of most vitamins and minerals meet recommended levels, many adolescents do not consume adequate amounts of several nutrients, including vitamin E, folate, magnesium, potassium, and fiber.
- Calcium intakes fall dramatically when children reach school age. Less than 40 percent of boys and 30 percent of girls between 6 and 11 years of age consume an adequate amount of calcium. The situation is even worse for adolescents: only about 10 percent of adolescent girls and 30 percent of adolescent boys get enough calcium.
- Iron-deficiency anemia is still the most common nutrient deficiency among American children, and the numbers continue to exceed the 2010 national health objective to reduce anemia.
- According to the Produce for Better Health Foundation, there are almost no children or teenagers eating the recommended number of fruit and vegetable servings per day. The data show that 96 percent do not meet current guidelines.

Poor nutrition among young people may have serious repercussions for both their present and future health. For example, an inadequate intake of antioxidants (from fruits and vegetables), as well as some vitamins and minerals, can increase the risk of cancer and heart disease later in life. In addition, inadequate nutrition can have a serious effect on bone growth and development. Children and adolescents with low intakes of protein, calcium, and other nutrients have a higher risk of fractures.

Although the majority of young people in the United States consume adequate amounts of calories, those calories are often "empty" ones, meaning that they do not include sufficient nutrients. Entries such as "Food Assistance" and "School Meals" look at what is being done to improve nutrition among children and adolescents.

Many studies also show a direct link between nutrition and academic performance. For example, increased participation in breakfast programs is associated with increased test scores, improved daily attendance, and better class participation. Optimal nutrition is necessary for optimal brain functioning, and being even slightly undernourished can affect academic performance and IQ scores. In particular, zinc, iron, and other nutrients are critical for brain development and function.

INFORMATION SOURCE

For those living in such a confusing environment, it is extremely helpful to have a source that young people can trust, a straightforward, easy-to-understand resource with everything they want to know about food and nutrition (even though they may not always know who to ask or what to ask). This encyclopedia is about just that. It is a comprehensive resource for information about everything from antibiotics in food to the zucchini at a farmers' market.

Food and Nutrition is a unique and important resource for today's youth (and the adults who

ABOUT THIS ENCYCLOPEDIA

This encyclopedia offers a comprehensive source of information about all aspects of food and nutrition. The 224 entries are arranged alphabetically in the first seven volumes. Readers looking for information on a specific topic can look directly in alphabetical order for that topic or can consult the detailed indexes in Volume 8. Readers with a more general interest are encouraged to consult the Thematic Table of Contents in this volume, which arranges the entries across nine categories.

Many entries are accompanied by illustrations and tables:

- Entries on specific foods—such as "Cheese" (see below) or "Yogurt"—feature tables with detailed nutritional data on energy (calories), protein, fat, and vitamins.
- Entries on particular nutrients—such as calcium, potassium, protein, and vitamins—include charts explaining the recommended daily intakes of the particular nutrient and how those needs differ depending on age and gender.
- Entries on particular world cuisines include maps. Where appropriate, arrows are used to indicate cultures that influenced the cuisine under discussion.

- Health entries on topics such as Digestion feature diagrams explaining bodily processes. Other diagrams are used to show, for example, how gene splicing is used to create new foods, how refrigerators keep food cool, and the molecular structure of different types of fats.

Each entry concludes with a list of sources for further study, both online and off, as well as a list of cross-references to more information within this set. Volume-specific indexes are included at the end of Volumes 1 through 7. Volume 8 contains a comprehensive index for all volumes, as well as specific indexes on foods and drinks, food-related diseases, and nutrients.

In Volume 8, readers will also find a glossary of terms and an expanded further reading list. Volume 8 also includes a collection of appendixes with tables that expand on the material within particular entries. For example, the entry "Fast Food" contains a selection of general nutritional information; in the appendix readers can compare a wider variety of additional fast foods from different companies. Likewise, while particular entries on subjects such as agriculture and hunger can only provide a brief overview of available data, the appendix offers a more comprehensive view.

CHEESE: NUTRITION INFORMATION

TYPE OF CHEESE	SERVING SIZE	ENERGY (kcal)	PROTEIN (g)	TOTAL FAT (g)	SODIUM (mg)	CALCIUM (mg)	VITAMIN B$_{12}$ (mcg)
American	1 slice (21 g)	38	5.17	1.47	300	144	0.16
Blue	1 oz. (28.35 g)	100	6.07	8.15	395	150	0.35
Brie	1 oz. (28.35 g)	95	5.88	7.85	178	52	0.47
Cheddar	1 slice (28 g)	113	6.97	9.28	174	202	0.23
Cottage	1 oz. (28.35 g)	20	3.50	0.29	115	17	0.18
Feta	1 oz. (28.35 g)	75	4.03	6.03	316	140	0.48
Mozzarella	1 oz. (28.35 g)	72	6.88	4.51	175	222	0.23
Parmesan	1 oz. (28.35 g)	122	10.90	8.11	433	314	0.64
Swiss	1 slice (28 g)	106	7.54	7.78	54	221	0.94

Notes: American (pasteurized process, low fat); cottage (low fat); mozzarella (part skim milk); Parmesan (grated).

Source: U.S. Department of Agriculture, Agricultural Research Service, USDA Nutrient Data Laboratory. USDA National Nutrient Database for Standard Reference, Release 19. 2006. Available from http://www.ars.usda.gov/nutrientdata.

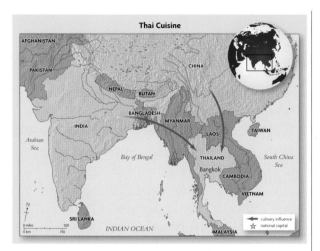

Entries on world cuisines include maps showing not only where the particular cuisine is located but also what other cuisines influenced it. For example, the red arrows on this map indicate that both Chinese and Indian cuisines were highly influential in the development of the cuisine of Thailand.

care about them and their health). With a truly encyclopedic approach to the universe of growing, choosing, cooking, eating, and enjoying food, these volumes combine the best parts of a food history and culture textbook, a cuisines-of-the-world cookbook, and a source of nutrition advice. It weaves together information about the past, the present, and even the future of food, nutrition, and well-being, covering exactly what young people need to know. The encyclopedia also covers environmental issues related to food and food production, such as sustainable agriculture and the slow food movement. It provides an amazing menu of food facts, tips, tidbits, and tasty recipes in more than 220 different entries (each with a book list and Web links for more detailed information). The entries are broken down into nine basics areas:

Cooking and Eating

Here readers can dig deeper into the science of cooking and the joy of eating to get answers to both everyday and more unusual questions, such as:

- How do microwaves make popcorn pop or heat up pizza?
- What is the difference between fast food and slow food?

Cuisines

In these entries, readers can appreciate the flavors of countries around the world and learn what elements are used to spice up traditional cuisines in places like England and Ethiopia, Italy and India, and Mexico and Morocco. Among the questions addressed are:

- How has American soul food been influenced by West African and Caribbean cuisines?
- What might be on the menu in a Brazilian, Greek, or Vietnamese restaurant?

Cultural and Social Aspects of Food

Readers can go behind the scenes and discover how food impacts every aspect of people's lives, including religious observations, jobs, and movies. This section looks at the following aspects, among others, of food in society:

- How do different religions affect what people are supposed to eat or not eat?
- How can one get a job in the food industry, such as chef or nutritionist?

Food Safety

These entries take a detailed look at what can happen when food is not cooked or stored properly. Questions about what people can do to keep from getting sick are addressed, including:

- Does hand washing before cooking food or eating a meal really matter?
- Will irradiating foods make them safe or unsafe to eat?

Foods and Drinks

These topics are like a tour through the aisles of a gigantic grocery store, with quick answers to important questions about the foods and drinks on the shelves, such as:

- Do diet foods and drinks actually help people lose weight in a healthful way?
- Are fruits and vegetables actually as good for you as parents claim?

Foods and Health

Readers will gain a deeper understanding of the phrase "you are what you eat" and discover why some foods can cause some people serious problems. For example:

- Are there foods and beverages that can cause—or cure—acne?
- Why are eating disorders, like anorexia and bulimia, such a problem for young people?

Nutrition

These entries share nutrition facts from A to zinc, exploring which nutrients do which jobs in our bodies. Young people can improve their health and energy levels by finding out:

- What foods and drinks help people perform better in sports?
- Do herbs and other supplements really do all that advertisements claim they do?

Production and Business of Food

Readers can find out where their food comes from before they order it in a restaurant or buy it off a supermarket shelf. They will discover answers to such questions as:

- How might global events have an impact on the cost of a gallon of milk?
- Do organic vegetables taste different or have more nutritional value than regular vegetables?

Weight and Weight Loss

Readers can get solid answers here to their questions about how to safely, and permanently, maintain a healthy weight, such as:

- What is body mass index (BMI), and how might it affect someone's body image?
- How can one tell the difference between a diet fad and a sensible eating plan?

With its broad perspective on food, nutrition, cooking, and eating, *Food and Nutrition* will be an inspiring and practical resource for adolescent readers. It offers the perfect combination of sensible nutrition solutions and global adventures in eating and cooking. The encyclopedia brings to the table exactly what the wisest nutrition and culinary experts have been preaching for years—balance, variety, moderation, and enjoyment. As the famous cookbook author and chef Julia Child said, "Eating well is one of life's greatest pleasures."

—Dayle Hayes

Volume Contents

Acid Indigestion

Acid indigestion is a common problem that principally affects adults but can also bother teenagers and younger children. Often called heartburn, acid indigestion causes a burning sensation in the chest, the neck, and the back of the throat. Despite its name, however, heartburn does not actually burn the heart.

CAUSES OF ACID INDIGESTION

Acid indigestion occurs when the band of muscles connecting the esophagus to the stomach, called the lower esophageal sphincter (LES), loosens and allows acidic stomach contents back into the esophagus. While digestion is taking place, the stomach churns food with a lot of force as it mixes the food with gastric acid. If the LES is not tight, the stomach pushes out its contents. Because the esophagus and throat do not have linings to protect them from the burn of stomach acid, acid indigestion can be painful. Some people have acid indigestion after almost every meal, but others feel its burn only occasionally.

Certain foods and beverages are more likely than others to cause acid indigestion. Chocolate,

COMMON FOODS THAT CAUSE INDIGESTION

- Chocolate
- Coffee
- Fried foods
- Orange juice
- Peppermint
- Soft drinks
- Tomato sauce

Fried foods, like these calamari, often cause acid indigestion.

peppermint, fried or fatty foods, coffee, and carbonated soft drinks weaken the LES and can cause indigestion. Smoking a cigarette also relaxes the LES. Some people are sensitive to orange juice, tomato sauce, or the combination of tomato sauce and high-fat cheese in foods such as pizza and baked pasta dishes.

Bending over or lying down after eating can lead to acid indigestion, especially after a large or fatty meal. Being overweight may also increase the occurrence of acid indigestion. Fat in the abdominal area puts pressure on the stomach and can force stomach contents to escape into the esophagus.

GETTING RELIEF

Relief from the burn of acid indigestion usually involves avoiding foods and beverages that cause pain. Some people have fewer symptoms if they eat smaller meals. Experts recommend avoiding eating from two to three hours before bedtime to give food a chance to leave the stomach before it is time to lie down. Athletes who have to bend over during sports can try eating a small, low-fat meal before games and competitions.

Several different over-the-counter medications can help relieve acid indigestion. The most common are antacids, which come in pill or liquid form and neutralize stomach acid to take away some of its burn. Other types of medications, such as histamine H_2-receptor antagonists and proton pump inhibitors, block the production of acid. Children, teenagers, and adults should consult a

doctor about which medication, if any, would best relieve their symptoms.

Frequent acid indigestion can be a symptom of gastroesophageal reflux disease (GERD), more commonly known as acid reflux. Repeated exposure to stomach acid can damage the lining of the esophagus and throat. If a change of diet does not work, a doctor may want to order tests to look for other causes.

FURTHER READING

Books and articles

Minocha, Ani, and Christine Adamec. *How to Stop Heartburn: Simple Ways to Heal Heartburn and Acid Reflux.* New York: Wiley, 2001.

Web sites

Johns Hopkins Gastroenterology and Hepatology Resource Center.
Information on the diagnosis, treatment, and prevention of digestive tract disorders.
http://hopkins-gi.nts.jhu.edu
Information Clearing House (NDDIC).
A government-sponsored Web site with information on acid indigestion and other problems of the gastrointestinal tract.
http://digestive.niddk.nih.gov

SEE ALSO

Digestion.

Acne

Acne is a skin condition affecting most teens, as well as some adults. Some teens have just a few pimples once in a while, but others suffer from more serious outbreaks that need to be controlled with prescription medications. Many people believe that certain foods, such as potato chips and chocolate, cause acne. In fact, these foods do not cause acne; nor do they make it worse.

WHY ACNE DEVELOPS

The skin is covered with small oil-secreting glands called sebaceous glands. Each gland is attached to a thin channel called a follicle, and each follicle contains a thin hair. Together the gland, follicle, and hair make up a pilosebaceous unit.

During puberty, the body produces higher amounts of hormones called androgens. These hormones signal sebaceous glands all over the body—but especially on the face, back, and chest—to become larger and secrete greater amounts of oil. The follicle of the pilosebaceous unit can become clogged, creating a plug, or comedo, that blocks the follicle opening. A bacteria strain, *Propionibacterium acnes* (*P. acnes*), flourishes in the warm, dark environment of the blocked follicle and sets off the process of infection, inflammation, and pimple formation.

An acne outbreak can involve several different types

SKIN CARE TIPS

- Wash face gently without scrubbing.
- Shampoo hair frequently.
- Avoid picking at pimples.
- Use oil-free cosmetics.
- Maintain a well-balanced diet.

of lesions. When the comedo forms a white bump under the skin surface, it is often called a whitehead. A comedo that opens at the surface of the skin is called a blackhead because its oily surface is exposed to oxygen, making it appear black. Pimples are reddened bumps on the skin surface that contain pus. Cysts are painful, pus-filled lumps that form below the skin surface.

Acne can be aggravated by certain behaviors. Cosmetics or moisturizers can cause follicles to become blocked and infected. Sports equipment that presses on the skin, such as helmets and straps, can trap sweat, oils, and dirt, causing blockages. Athletes who do not wash their face shortly after a practice or game may find that their acne increases.

Acne also may become more severe owing to the stress of exams, a heavy workload, or social pressures. Girls may find that their acne worsens several days before menstruation starts, because of changes in hormone levels.

DIET AND ACNE

It is commonly believed that chocolate and fatty foods cause acne or make it worse. The truth is that most foods, even the least nutritious, do not have any effect on acne. Research does occasionally suggest a connection between diet and acne, however.

For example, in 2005 a study found a relationship between the ingestion of dairy products and acne during the teenage years.

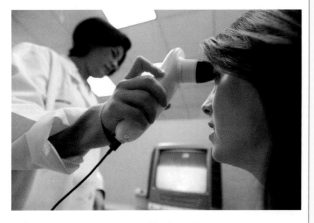

A doctor uses a device called a sebumeter to measure the amount of oil on a patient's skin.

However, this connection needs to be studied more closely before definitive conclusions can be drawn. In the meantime, although plenty of books and Web sites blame diet for acne flare-ups, scientifically proved conclusions are extremely scarce.

OVERVIEW OF ACNE TREATMENTS

Many acne treatments are used directly on the skin. Products containing benzoyl peroxide help kill *P. acnes* and dry the skin. Salicylic acid and sulfur, two other common ingredients, help eliminate blackheads and whiteheads. Prescription products are generally stronger than over-the-counter brands.

A physician or dermatologist may prescribe oral medications for more serious cases of acne. Oral antibiotics help reduce inflammation by controlling the growth of bacteria. Medications that contain retinoids related to vitamin A make oil glands smaller. (Although these medications are related to vitamin A, their active ingredient is not found in food.)

Although acne is an undesirable inconvenience, most cases of acne last for only a few years during puberty. Over-the-counter and prescription acne treatments are quite effective at controlling serious flare-ups.

FURTHER READING

Books and articles

Ceaser, Jennifer. *Everything You Need to Know about Acne: A Helping Book for Teens.* New York: Rosen, 2002.

Web sites

Skin Care Physicians: AcneNet.

A comprehensive acne information resource from the American Academy of Dermatologists.

http://www.skincarephysicians.com/acnenet

SEE ALSO

Human Growth and Development; Hygiene.

Additives

The term *additive* refers to any substance that is added to food. Additives are essential ingredients in modern food production. They keep bread from molding quickly, salt from clumping, and mayonnaise from separating; they improve the nutritional benefits of cereals and pastas; and they keep packaged cookies crunchy and prepackaged salads crisp. Without additives, people would not be able to enjoy seasonal foods year-round; nor could they consume the wide variety of canned or packaged foods generally available today. Additives extend shelf life, improve taste and appearance, and enable food manufacturers to turn out safe, consistent products.

Additives include preservatives, artificial and natural colors and flavors, vitamins, minerals, and other chemicals. They come in many different forms, from those as simple and familiar as salt, sugar, baking soda, and yeast to those as complex as ethoxylated monodiglycerides and butylated hydroxyanisole (BHA). All additives used in food production in the United States, Europe, and other developed countries are tightly regulated. Still, some consumer groups remain wary about the effects that additives may be having on human health—particularly the health of children.

SELECTED TYPES OF ADDITIVES

- Antioxidants
- Artificial sweeteners
- Color retention agents
- Coloring
- Emulsifiers
- Firming agents
- Flavor enhancers
- Food acids
- Gelling agents
- Glazing agents
- Improving agents
- Mineral salts
- Preservatives
- Seasonings
- Stabilizers
- Sweeteners
- Thickeners
- Vegetable gums

HISTORY OF ADDITIVES

Humans have used additives to help make food taste better or last longer since the earliest days of civilization. Research suggests that prehistoric humans

A Japanese fish dealer carries baskets of salted salmon and tuna on a bamboo pole in 1865. Salt is one of the world's oldest additives.

knew how to use certain additives, such as salt, to help preserve meat. Ancient Greeks burned sulfur when making wine, to help preserve it as it aged; and there is evidence of food coloring used in Egypt in 1500 BCE.

Some of the most common and simplest preservatives have been around for thousands of years. One of the oldest is salt, which is still used to preserve meats and fish. Sugar has long been used as a preservative, as has vinegar, which is used for pickling. Herbs and spices have been employed for ages to improve flavor and change the texture of foods. Once refrigeration and other technological advances arrived, however, additives began to evolve. In the early twenty-first century, more than 3,000 additives are used regularly in the U.S. food supply.

WHAT DO ADDITIVES DO?

Additives have many functions. Some are used to add or change color, and thus make prepared or processed food look more attractive. Without color additives, for example, colas would not be brown, mint chip ice cream would not be green, and margarine would not have a buttery yellow color but would instead be off-white.

Some additives help preserve food and extend shelf life by stopping the growth of microorganisms; others do so by preventing food from reacting with oxygen in the air or with certain metals used in packaging. Still other additives help improve the texture of some foods, making them smoother, as in the case of blended soups, or crisper, as in the case of prepared vegetables.

Additives not only sweeten or otherwise flavor food but sometimes impart additional nutrients. Omega-3, for example, is a fatty acid that is believed to improve brain function and reduce heart disease, and it is sometimes added to foods such as eggs and dairy products, orange juice, and butter substitutes. Folic acid, an important nutrient that helps prevent birth defects and has been shown to help protect brain function in older people, is another very useful food additive. In the United States, food manufacturers are required by law to add folic acid to many breads, cereals, and pastas to help meet this nutritional need. Additives are not considered "food," however, even though they can impart nutrients. They are simply considered a part of a food product.

There are different categories of additives: they can be direct or indirect, and they can be artificial or natural. Direct additives are added to a

Without additives, the margarine in this tub would be off-white, not yellow.

food product for a specific purpose. These additives are usually identified on the product label. One common example would be an artificial sweetener, such as sucralose. Indirect additives are substances that come into contact with food during production or through packaging. These additives are not always labeled.

Artificial additives are made from chemical compounds, whereas natural additives are derived from natural products, such as the reddish-purple coloring that comes from beets. Although the term *natural* might have positive connotations for some, natural additives are not necessarily better than artificial additives. In fact, natural additives can sometimes be more difficult to use because they are not always as consistent as human-made ones.

REGULATION OF ADDITIVES

Although most additives used today are harmless, some have been shown to cause adverse effects.

Berries of the pokeweed plant were once commonly used to make red dyes, and the food industry still uses pokeweed as a natural food coloring.

COMMON ADDITIVES AND THEIR USES

Additive function: impart or maintain desired consistency of food
Used in: baked goods, cake mixes, salad dressings, ice cream, processed cheese, coconut, table salt
Examples: alginates, lecithin, mono- and diglycerides, methyl cellulose, carrageenan, glyceride, pectin, guar gum, sodium aluminosilicate

Additive function: improve and maintain nutritive value of food
Used in: flour, bread, biscuits, breakfast cereals, pasta, margarine, milk, iodized salt, gelatin desserts
Examples: vitamins A and D, thiamine, niacin, riboflavin, pyridoxine, folic acid, ascorbic acid, calcium carbonate, zinc oxide, iron

Additive function: maintain freshness
Used in: bread, cheese, crackers, frozen and dried fruit, margarine, lard, potato chips, cake mixes, meat
Examples: propionic acid and its salts, ascorbic acid, butylated hydroxyanisole (BHA), butylated hydroxytoluene (BHT), benzoates, sodium nitrite, citric acid

Additive function: produce light texture; control acidity and alkalinity
Used in: cakes, cookies, quick breads, crackers, butter, chocolates, soft drinks
Examples: yeast, sodium bicarbonate, citric acid, fumaric acid, phosphoric acid, lactic acid, tartrates

Additive function: enhance flavor or impart desired color
Used in: spice cake, gingerbread, soft drinks, yogurt, soup, confections, baked goods, cheeses, jams, gum
Examples: cloves, ginger, fructose, aspartame, saccharin, FD&C Red No. 40, monosodium glutamate, caramel, annatto, limonene, turmeric

Source: Food and Drug Administration, International Food Information Council.

The chief concerns about additives are whether they cause allergies, whether they are toxic (if consumed in large or small amounts), and whether they are carcinogenic.

Worldwide, groups such as the World Health Organization (WHO) and the United Nations Food and Agriculture Organization (FAO) monitor additives, and most countries have their own food safety organizations as well. In the United States, the U.S. Food and Drug Administration (FDA) is charged with monitoring the safety of proposed and existing additives.

Legislation regarding food safety began in the early twentieth century, with the Federal Food and Drug Act of 1906, also known as the Pure Food Law. It prohibited the sale of "adulterated" food and drugs across state lines. Then, in 1938, the Federal Food, Drug, and Cosmetic Act (FDCA) gave the FDA the legal authority to monitor food, ingredients, and additives. This law also required the truthful labeling of ingredients, and it placed the responsibility for identifying "unsafe" additives or ingredients with the government.

Effective federal regulation of additives began in the 1950s, as industrial food production became established in the United States and packaged convenience foods became a part of everyday American life. In 1958 the Food Additives Amendment to the FDCA required that the FDA approve any additive before it could be included in a food product. Two years later the Color Additives Amendment required that all natural and artificial coloring agents be tested for safety, and it stated that coloring could not be used to mask inferior or tainted foods. With both amendments, the burden of proof shifted: the government no longer had to show that an additive was unsafe; rather, the manufacturer now had to prove that the additive was safe.

Two classes of additives were exempt from these laws. One included familiar substances, such as salt and caffeine, which experts believed to be "generally recognized as safe" (GRAS). The other class included substances that had already been approved by the FDA. Both classes of exempt substances can be reviewed in light of new scientific evidence or safety standards. In 1969, for example, artificial sweeteners known as cyclamates, which had GRAS status since the 1950s, were removed from the market because this class of sweeteners had been shown to cause tumors in lab rats.

One of the key aspects of the amendments of 1958 and 1960 is known as the Delaney Clause. It specifically addresses cancer and additives. This is one of the most restrictive aspects of federal law regarding additives, and thus the one that modern-day food manufacturers are mostly likely to try to resist. A 1996 law, the Food Quality Protection Act, eliminated the Delaney Clause in the case of pesticide residues.

Although the FDA's regulation of food, ingredients, and additives is rigorous, it is not without its faults. Some consumer watchdog groups, most notably the Center for Science in the Public Interest, maintain that the FDA does not do enough to ensure that additives do not cause harm.

Even something as "natural" as packaged lettuce requires additives such as antimicrobials to keep the food fresh.

PROBLEM ADDITIVES

Even when an additive is generally deemed safe, it may still cause problems for some people, with physical reactions ranging from minor itching or hives to, in a small number of cases, death. Sulfites, for example, are a common type of preservative that are "generally recognized as safe," but they can be harmful to people with asthma. The FDA banned the use of sulfites on fresh fruits and vegetables in 1986 to help mitigate the problem, and the law requires that sulfites be listed on the product label. Some people are allergic to a type of food coloring known as FD&C Yellow No. 5, or tartrazine; others are sensitive to monosodium glutamate (MSG), which is commonly used to enhance the flavor of food.

A few additives approved by the FDA are controversial. Some studies have shown that nitrites and nitrates, which are used to prevent botulism in cured meats such as bacon, can cause cancer in lab animals. Proponents argue that the risk of death or negative health effects from botulism is the more serious issue, outweighing any possible risk of cancer.

Recent studies on additives are tackling the difficult problem of safe additives that become toxic when used in combination. A study in 2005, for instance, showed that combinations like MSG and blue food coloring or aspartame and yellow food coloring can be toxic, especially to children, even though the additives are nontoxic when used independently. This is an especially important realm of research, as many food products have a dozen or more additives in them.

Although people often worry about the potentially harmful nature of additives such as sulfites and MSG, even the safest of additives can cause problems if consumed in excess. For example, in the United States, most people consume 10 times more sugar than any other additive, and salt is the second most commonly consumed additive. Most food products contain two or more different types of sugar and salt. Nutritionists and public health experts alike are quick to point out that sugar and salt can be harmful, precipitating

Unregulated Additives

The FDA does a good—if not perfect—job of regulating the additives used in the U.S. food supply. In some countries, regulations and practices are not as stringent. According to a May 2007 story in the *Wall Street Journal*, formaldehyde, which has been shown to cause cancer, is commonly used as a food additive in Indonesia. A study from 2005 found that more than half of the various food items sampled tested positive for formaldehyde. Another artificial coloring additive, called "Sudan Red," is also associated with cancer, but it is used in various countries to enhance the color of drinks or impart a red color to eggs (by being added to chicken feed). These additives are not listed on labels, and individual purveyors or farmers are not likely to inform customers that they are being used.

ABOVE: An Indonesian protester at a demonstration in 2006 against the widespread use of formalin, a type of formaldehyde, as a food preservative.

diseases such as type 2 diabetes and high blood pressure, respectively.

Additives are neither wholly good nor wholly bad. The key, most experts agree, is moderation. Additive-rich foods should be monitored. Consumers—particularly individuals with special sensitivities and allergies—should pay close attention to product labels. As much as possible, people are encouraged to eat fresh fruits and vegetables and minimally processed meats and grains, and to eat a wide variety of foods, thus avoiding the consumption of too much of any one additive.

FURTHER READING

Books and articles

Guinn, Bob. "Are the Chemicals We Eat Safe?" *Orlando Sentinel,* May 15, 2007.

Murphy, Kate. "Do Food Additives Subtract from Health?" *Business Week*, May 6, 1996. Available from http://www.businessweek.com/1996/19/b3474101.htm.

Winter, Ruth. *A Consumer's Dictionary of Food Additives.* New York: Three Rivers, 2004.

Zamiska, Nicholas. "Unsafe Food Additives Across Asia Feed Fears." *Wall Street Journal,* May 9, 2007.

Web sites

Center for Food Safety and Applied Nutrition: Food Additives.

A pro-additive primer from the FDA.

http://www.cfsan.fda.gov/~lrd/foodaddi.html

Center for Science in the Public Interest (CSPI): Food Additives.

An additive-wary primer from a consumer group.

http://www.cspinet.org/reports/chemcuisine.htm

CNN Food Central: Resources: Common Food Additives.

A list of common food additives, with their applications and possible side effects.

http://www.cnn.com/FOOD/resources/food.for.thought/additives/table.html

U.S. Food and Drug Administration: Everything Added to Food in the United States (EAFUS).

A list of the more than 3,000 additives approved for use in food.

http://www.foodsafety.gov/~dms/eafus.html

SEE ALSO

Allergies; Antibiotics in Foods; Herbs; Labeling; Legislation and Food; Omega-3; Processed Food; Salt, Table; Sugars; Taste; Tastes and Flavors Industry.

Agricultural Subsidy

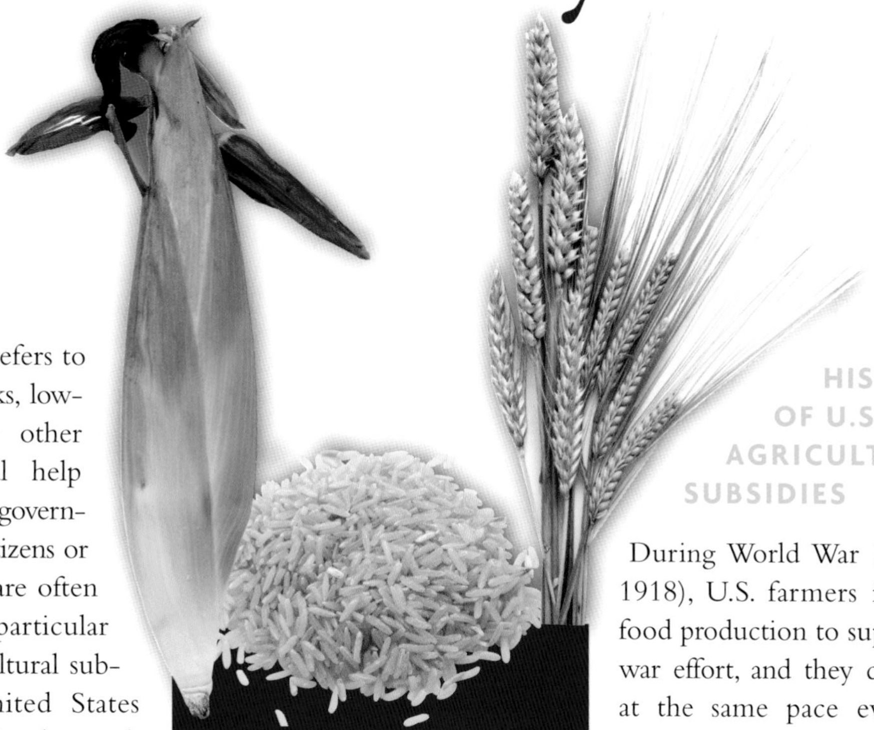

The term *subsidy* refers to payments, tax breaks, low-interest loans, or other types of financial help that are given by governments to private citizens or groups. Subsidies are often used to support particular industries. Agricultural subsidies in the United States began with a simple goal: to support farmers through times of drought, disaster, or hardship, and thereby secure a reliable food supply. Safe and affordable food production is vital not only for the livelihood of farmers but also for the health and survival of the entire country. However, as farming and food production in the United States have evolved and become part of a global economy, agricultural subsidies have become a complicated political issue.

MAJOR SUBSIDIZED CROPS

- Barley
- Corn
- Cotton
- Grain sorghum
- Oats
- Rice
- Soybeans
- Wheat

HISTORY OF U.S. AGRICULTURAL SUBSIDIES

During World War I (1914–1918), U.S. farmers increased food production to support the war effort, and they continued at the same pace even after the war had ended. This overproduction resulted in a glut of produce on the market, which caused a drop in food prices. Low prices, in turn, forced some farmers out of business. The government stepped in to help stabilize the farming economy so that farmers could stay in the business of producing food.

Subsidies increased considerably amid the intense economic hardships of the Great Depression. Government agencies such as the Farm Security Administration, created in 1935, distributed agricultural subsidies to reduce unemployment and stabilize the industry. In addition, in order to control overproduction, some farmers were paid to stop producing food altogether. In the 1930s, one in four Americans worked on a farm, so the subsidies directly benefited a large number of Americans.

Once subsidies began, however, they were hard to stop. In the twenty-first century, U.S. subsidies are focused on five main crops—corn, soybeans, rice, cotton, and wheat. Farmers involved in these crops receive 93 percent of agricultural subsidies. Of the $164 billion in federal aid handed out to farms between 1995 and 2005, just 10 percent of farms received nearly three-quarters of the money, while six in ten farmers received no subsidies at all.

Because many subsidies come in the form of direct payments based on output, farmers cultivating certain subsidized crops are encouraged to produce as much as possible, without consideration of economic fallout, such as overproduction. For example, the Farm Security and Rural Investment Act of 2002, better known as the Farm Bill, provides that soybean farmers be paid an additional 44 cents for every bushel of soybeans they produce. The bill also guarantees that farmers will receive a

THE NEW ZEALAND EXPERIMENT

In 1984 the government of New Zealand decided to eliminate agricultural subsidies. New Zealand was one of the first developed countries to do so, and it remains one of the few today. After the expected protests and turmoil in the immediate wake of the transition, New Zealand farmers adjusted to the new free-market system. They became more efficient, more diverse in their production, and more sensitive to consumers' needs and demands. By many accounts, the New Zealand farming industry is as healthy as it has ever been.

minimum price of $5.80 per bushel, regardless of the demand.

PROS AND CONS

Those who favor agricultural subsidies argue that farming is a special sector of the economy and deserves to have federal support. Because harsh economic realities and unforeseen events such as droughts make farming a difficult profession, farmers might eventually abandon their fields and move into a more profitable sector if they did not receive subsidies. Without federal support, proponents argue, the food supply is in danger. Subsidies also keep prices low for staple crops like such as corn or soybeans; and low prices in turn reduce costs for food manufacturers, distributors, and the entire food industry. Thus, all consumers benefit from agricultural subsidies, in the form of affordable industrial food products. Still other proponents argue that subsidies help preserve a landscape and a rural way of life associated with simpler times.

Those critical of agricultural subsidies say that they encourage the overproduction of food, driving down prices, and, ironically, creating a need for even more aid to address the drop

A farm couple waiting outside a Farm Security Administration office in 1938. Photographed by Dorothea Lange.

A farmer planting corn in Batavia, Illinois. Critics argue that federal subsidies encourage farmers to plant subsidized crops at the expense of other foods.

Advances in biotechnology have created drought-resistant seeds, for example, resulting in ever-increasing crop growth, even in years with little rainfall. Meanwhile, many economists point out that although agricultural subsidies do lower food prices, the subsidies themselves come directly from taxpayers; in other words, consumers might save money in the grocery store but they will have to pay it back at tax time.

Other critics argue that the subsidies do not actually benefit the small-scale farmers who are evoked when lobbyists and politicians mention the "family farm" or "rural America." Most subsidies are funneled to already wealthy agribusinesses, and the real savings are passed along the industrial food chain, to grain brokers and processors of prepackaged foods that use corn or soy products. In addition, they point out that industrial farming creates a landscape quite unlike the rural American family farm.

in farmers' income. Some argue that the original need for subsidies—to protect farmers from unexpected catastrophes—no longer exists.

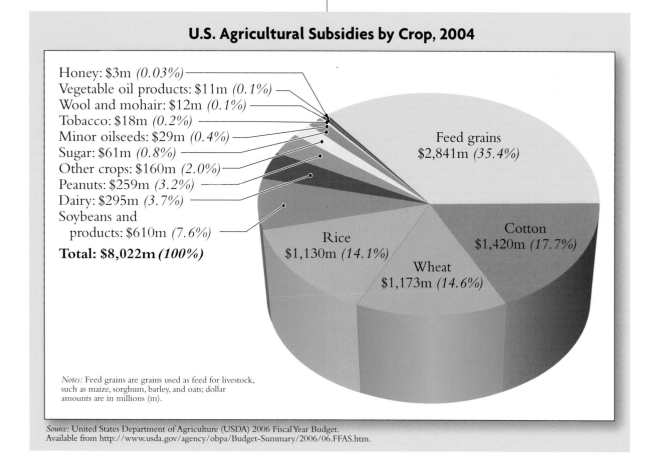

U.S. Agricultural Subsidies by Crop, 2004

Honey: $3m *(0.03%)*
Vegetable oil products: $11m *(0.1%)*
Wool and mohair: $12m *(0.1%)*
Tobacco: $18m *(0.2%)*
Minor oilseeds: $29m *(0.4%)*
Sugar: $61m *(0.8%)*
Other crops: $160m *(2.0%)*
Peanuts: $259m *(3.2%)*
Dairy: $295m *(3.7%)*
Soybeans and
products: $610m *(7.6%)*
Total: $8,022m *(100%)*

Feed grains
$2,841m *(35.4%)*

Cotton
$1,420m *(17.7%)*

Rice
$1,130m *(14.1%)*

Wheat
$1,173m *(14.6%)*

Notes: Feed grains are grains used as feed for livestock, such as maize, sorghum, barley, and oats; dollar amounts are in millions (m).

Source: United States Department of Agriculture (USDA) 2006 Fiscal Year Budget.
Available from http://www.usda.gov/agency/obpa/Budget-Summary/2006/06.FFAS.htm.

Agricultural subsidies have a global impact as well. In order to support sufficient price levels for domestic farmers, the U.S. government withholds food from the domestic market and dumps it on the world market at a price below the cost of production. This lowers the global price of the food, severely tipping the trade scales in favor of the United States. For farmers in developing countries, this artificial pricing can be devastating because they are not able to compete. Agricultural subsidies have thus become a sticking point in international trade negotiations.

Subsidies, environmentalists argue, also discourage farmers from practicing crop rotation, which keeps the soil healthy. Subsidies largely determine what is or is not grown; currently, this primarily means that soy, corn, wheat, and cotton are planted rather than unsubsidized crops. Single-crop production can quickly strip land of its nutrients, requiring increased amounts of artificial fertilizer, which can further damage the environment if the fertilizer reaches the water supply.

Some public health experts argue that the overproduction of subsidized grains has led to an unhealthy level of grain-based products in the American diet. Although government health agencies advise people to consume five servings per day of fresh fruits and vegetables, national agricultural policies do not appear to support that recommendation. According to one academic, fruits and vegetables receive roughly one-tenth of 1 percent of each subsidized dollar.

In the United States, there are efforts underway to change the state of agricultural subsidies. Similar efforts are underway in other countries that practice subsidies, including those in the European Union. These changes are intended to benefit public health, global trade, and the farmers themselves, for whom agricultural subsidies were created nearly a century ago.

FURTHER READING

Books and articles

Barrionuevo, Alexei, and Keith Bradsher. "Sometimes a Bumper Crop Is Too Much of a Good Thing." *New York Times,* December 9, 2005.

England, Vaudine. "Shorn of Subsidies, New Zealand Farmers Thrive," *International Herald Tribune,* July 2, 2005. Available from http://www.iht.com/articles/2005/07/01/news/zealand.php.

Gardner, B. L. *American Agriculture in the Twentieth Century: How It Flourished and What It Cost.* Cambridge, MA: Harvard University Press; 2002.

Web sites

Environmental Working Group: Farm Subsidy Database.

This database identifies recipients of farm subsidies in the United States.

http://farm.ewg.org/farm

Rudd Center for Food Policy and Obesity: Food Subsidies.

Information on books, papers, and Web sites related to food subsidies and the effect on diet and health.

http://www.yaleruddcenter.org/default.aspx?id=170

U.S. Department of Agriculture: 2002 Farm Bill.

Detailed information on the 2002 Farm Bill from the Economic Research Service of the USDA.

http://www.ers.usda.gov/Features/FarmBill

Washington Post: Harvesting Cash.

A digest of news articles on farm subsidies, which identify domestic issues.

http://www.washingtonpost.com/wp-srv/nation/interactives/farmaid

SEE ALSO

Farming, Industrial; Farming, Traditional; Food Prices; Legislation and Food.

Alcohol

Alcohol in the human diet typically refers to a drink or brew containing ethyl alcohol (ethanol). Alcoholic drinks are produced by one of two processes: fermentation or distillation. Fermentation causes fruit, grains, or vegetables to partially rot and become liquid. In this process, sugars or carbohydrates in the food are converted to alcohol. Examples include fermenting grapes to make wine and brewing mixed fermented grains to produce beer. The distillation of fermented fruit, vegetable, or grain mixtures involves heating the fermented liquid to produce spirits such as gin, vodka, rum, or whiskey.

The liquid produced by either of these processes will exhibit distinctive flavors depending on the food substance used. These liquids will also contain varying percentages of ethyl alcohol, which may be intoxicating. The distillation process concentrates the alcoholic content, so distilled beverages have higher percentages of ethanol than fermented beverages (see table, Alcoholic Content in Some Beverages).

After someone drinks an alcoholic beverage, the alcohol is absorbed from the stomach and intestine into the bloodstream. The alcohol is then carried very quickly to the brain and throughout the body. Alcohol remains in the body until it is metabolized (or broken down) by the liver. It is released from the body through urine, perspiration, and breath.

HISTORY OF ALCOHOL

The use of alcohol in the human diet, and in human society, dates back tens of thousands of years. It was almost

---

ALCOHOL ABUSE STATISTICS

- One-quarter of all emergency room admissions, one-third of all suicides, and more than half of all homicides and incidents of domestic violence are alcohol-related.
- Heavy drinking contributes to illness in each of the top three causes of death: heart disease, cancer, and stroke.
- Almost half of all traffic fatalities are alcohol-related.
- Between 48 and 64 percent of people who die in fires have blood alcohol levels indicating intoxication.

Source: National Council on Alcoholism and Drug Dependence. Available from http://www.ncadd.org.

Winemakers enjoy some of their harvested grapes before they are put through a wine press in Salemi, Sicily.

certainly discovered by accident, perhaps when someone first sampled the juice that came from fermenting fruit or grain. Since prehistoric times, alcohol has been used in religious ceremonies and has been prized for its value in medicinal, nutritional, and antiseptic applications. In contemporary times it is central to cooking and eating, both as an ingredient in foods and as an accompaniment to meals.

Although the first human consumption of alcohol most likely occurred by accident, researchers have found evidence in late Stone Age jugs that Neolithic humans had begun to create fermented beverages intentionally by around 8000 BCE. It was also around this time that humans began to develop settled communities based on agriculture and domesticated animals. As techniques to produce alcohol developed, so did the technologies that allowed the production of alcoholic drinks such as wine.

The eastern Mediterranean region, where grapes grew wild, was the likely birthplace of wine making. Egyptian pictographs dating from approximately 4000 BCE show wine among the possessions of the Egyptians. Other early alcoholic beverages were probably made from honey or fermented berries. In Egyptian and other societies, these beverages were important as offerings to gods, for social occasions, and for trade. Early records indicate that wine and beer were frequently used as a form of money to obtain other necessities. Much later, during the Middle Ages in Europe, ale was often used as a form of payment.

In Greece, before wine became a staple around 2000 BCE, a fermented beverage of honey and water, which in English is called mead, was popular. In China, some of the earliest records indicate the importance of alcohol (often made from fermented rice) in both religious rituals and civic ceremonies.

ALCOHOLIC CONTENT IN SOME BEVERAGES

BEVERAGE	ALCOHOL CONTENT (%)
Beer (lager or ale)	3.2 to 4.5
Wine (table or sparkling)	7.0 to 14.0
Fortified wine	14.0 to 24.0
Brandy	40.0 to 43.0
Whiskey	40.0 to 75.0
Vodka	40.0 to 50.0
Gin	40.0 to 48.5
Rum	40.0 to 95.0
Tequila	45.0 to 50.5

Note: This table shows the percentage of alcohol in one drink, defined as 12 ounces (375 ml) of beer, 5 ounces (150 ml) of wine, or 1.5 ounces (45 ml) of distilled spirits.

ALCOHOL AND HEALTH

From earliest times, societies have had regulations prohibiting intoxication. Alcohol has always been associated with dangers to health: both the health of the individual and, because of the lawlessness that often follows extreme drunkenness, the health of the community. In addition to endangering people's health, excessive alcohol consumption severely affects their movements, vision, and judgment. Inebriated ("drunk") people often do things they would not normally do—sometimes involving violence or thoughtless behavior that can jeopardize themselves and others.

Evidence suggests that the moderate use of alcohol in the modern diet is not detrimental to health. In fact, several medical studies in the late twentieth century showed that alcohol consumption in small amounts may actually contribute to the health of a normal adult. In tests, both men and women who consumed limited amounts of alcohol have had a lower incidence of heart disease and stroke than people who either were heavy drinkers or did not drink alcohol at all. Researchers theorize that this results from alcohol's ability to raise levels of high-density lipoprotein (HDL, or "good cholesterol") in a person's body, thereby providing protection against heart disease. Alcohol has also been found to help guard against the kind of blood clotting that could block arteries and lead to heart attacks or strokes.

All these studies stress, however, that any of alcohol's potential benefits to health would result only from moderate drinking (meaning no more than two drinks a day for men and one drink for women), and that excessive drinking carries very serious health risks, including damage to the heart, liver, and brain. Moreover, in women even moderate drinking has been associated with increased risk of breast cancer. Women who are pregnant are advised not to drink alcohol because of the potential of harming the fetus. Drinking alcohol causes behavioral changes and can impair judgment, perception, and motor skills. In the United States, alcohol plays a role in approximately one-half of all fatal automobile accidents.

Wine is frequently used in cooking; the alcohol evaporates during the cooking process, leaving only the flavor behind.

Alcohol Use among Young People in the United States, 2005

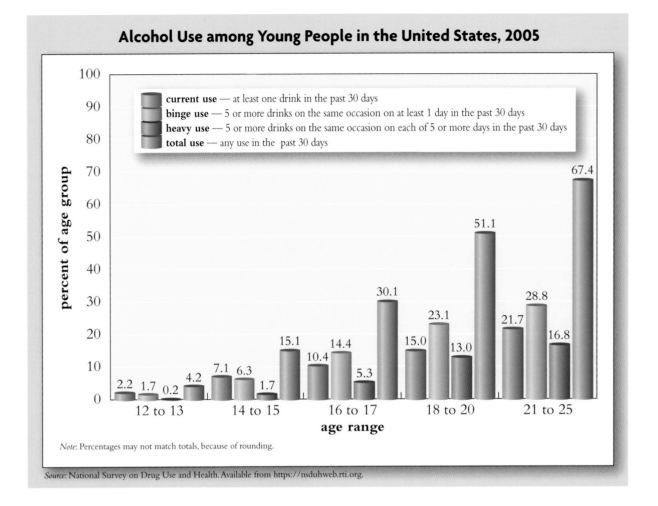

current use — at least one drink in the past 30 days
binge use — 5 or more drinks on the same occasion on at least 1 day in the past 30 days
heavy use — 5 or more drinks on the same occasion on each of 5 or more days in the past 30 days
total use — any use in the past 30 days

Note: Percentages may not match totals, because of rounding.

Source: National Survey on Drug Use and Health. Available from https://nsduhweb.rti.org.

These factors, especially when combined with the increasing problems of binge drinking and underage drinking, pose serious social issues.

Alcohol's potential benefits to health should be weighed very carefully against its potentially harmful effects.

FURTHER READING

Books and articles

Hanson, David J. *Preventing Alcohol Abuse: Alcohol, Culture, and Control.* Westport, CT: Praeger, 1995.

Web sites

Harvard School of Public Health: Alcohol.
Information on risks, possible health benefits, and general use and effects of alcohol.
http://www.hsph.harvard.edu/nutritionsource/alcohol.html

National Youth Violence Prevention Center: Teens and Alcohol.
Statistical information on the prevalence of alcohol use by teenagers. Also provides helpful links about teenage alcohol abuse and tips on recognizing the signs of a drinking problem.
http://www.safeyouth.org/scripts/teens/alcohol.asp

SEE ALSO

Fermentation; Heart Disease; Juice; Legislation and Food; Movies, Television, and Food; Religion and Food.

Allergies

An allergic reaction occurs when a person's immune system responds to a substance in an exaggerated, abnormal way. The substance that causes the allergic reaction is called an allergen. In theory, any food can cause an allergic reaction, but most allergic reactions are caused by one of a small number of foods (see box, Common Food Allergies). Symptoms can range from mild to severe, and in very rare cases allergies can be fatal for people whose bodies react violently to a

COMMON FOOD ALLERGIES

Up to 90 percent of food-allergic reactions are triggered by one of the following foods:

- Eggs
- Fish
- Milk
- Peanuts
- Shellfish
- Soy
- Tree nuts
- Wheat

particular food or another kind of allergen.

Anyone can have an allergy to a food, and although allergies can develop at any time, most of them develop in childhood. Commonly, children develop allergies very early in life (there is no clear evidence that they are born with allergies), and many lose their allergies as they get older. Around 1 child in 20 has food allergies, with the figure dropping to 1 in 100 in adults. It is not unusual for babies to be allergic to cow's milk, and infants are also often

One relatively widespread allergy is to shellfish, such as these lobsters. Shellfish allergies tend to persist throughout a person's lifetime, and allergic reactions to shellfish can be serious.

allergic to eggs, soy, and wheat. In general, allergies to nuts, fish, peanuts, and shellfish tend to last a lifetime. Although it is not common, a person who has eaten a particular food for many years without any problem may suddenly develop an allergy to it. The reasons for this are not fully understood, however.

The term *allergy* is often used incorrectly. An allergy can be confused with a condition known as food intolerance, which is a reaction to food that has different physiological symptoms. A food allergy is an almost immediate reaction from the body's immune system. A food intolerance, on the other hand, does not involve an allergic response from the immune system; it results when a person's digestive system lacks an enzyme that it needs to properly digest a certain food. For instance, someone who has difficulty digesting milk is lactose intolerant, meaning that he or she lacks the enzyme needed to digest the sugars in milk properly. This intolerance causes symptoms such as abdominal pain and gas. It is not the same as having an allergy to milk, however.

ALLERGIES AND THE BODY

An allergic reaction occurs when the body responds as if the proteins in a foreign substance, such as a food, are poisonous or toxic. When the food is eaten, the body creates antibodies to destroy the proteins. After the first exposure, the antibodies identify the substance every time it is eaten (in the case of food) and cause the immune system to react against it. This can cause a variety of reactions, from a mild tingling in the mouth to severe breathing difficulties, and in very rare cases allergies can cause death (see box, Symptoms of Food Allergy). Research published in the *Journal of Allergy and Clinical Immunology* in 2001 indicates that 150 people die each year in the United States from food-related allergic reactions, and many more suffer from severe reactions.

The allergy antibody is a type called immunoglobulin E, or IgE. These antibodies act as sensors for mast cells, which are large immune system cells, located mostly in the innermost layer of the skin. Mast cells contain a number of chemicals, including histamine, which they can release when triggered. The chemicals fight against bacterial infection and parasites, causing an inflammatory response. When the allergen is eaten, the particular IgE antibodies that identify the proteins in that food send chemical signals to trigger the mast cells, which then release their histamine (and other irritants), initiating an allergic reaction. All allergies cause this sequence of events. If the allergen is a food, a person will have

How an Allergic Reaction Takes Place

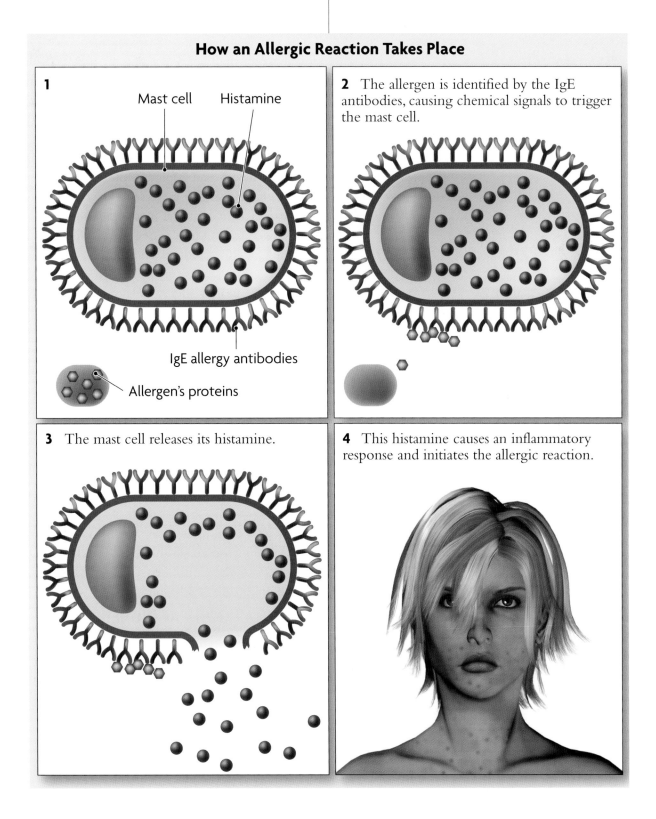

1

Mast cell   Histamine

IgE allergy antibodies

Allergen's proteins

2 The allergen is identified by the IgE antibodies, causing chemical signals to trigger the mast cell.

3 The mast cell releases its histamine.

4 This histamine causes an inflammatory response and initiates the allergic reaction.

SYMPTOMS OF FOOD ALLERGY

An allergic reaction usually happens within one to two minutes of eating a food. Any or all of the following symptoms can occur as a result of a food allergy, sometimes as a mild reaction:

- Tingling sensation in the mouth and lips
- Swelling of tongue and throat
- Rash, anywhere on the body, often in the groin
- Eczema
- Hives and swelling, particularly of throat and face
- Vomiting
- Abdominal cramps
- Diarrhea
- Wheezing and difficulty in breathing
- Drop in blood pressure (a sign of immune-induced shock)
- Loss of consciousness

an allergic reaction each time he or she eats that food. In extreme cases, even touching wrappers or other substances that have been in contact with the food triggers a reaction.

Allergic reactions include swelling or hives, dizziness, confusion, and a drop in blood pressure (see box, Symptoms of Food Allergy). One unusually violent, life-threatening response is called anaphylaxis. When a person goes into anaphylactic shock, he or she will have had an almost immediate and severe reaction, including breathing problems, loss of consciousness, and a severe drop in blood pressure. This kind of reaction is rare, but it requires immediate emergency treatment. An injection of the hormone epinephrine, also known as adrenaline, works to reverse the effects of anaphylaxis, but it does not cure the allergy. Because of the severity of anaphylactic shock, people who are likely to suffer a severe allergic reaction to a food (or anything else) need to carry supplies of injectable adrenaline, and they often wear a bracelet to alert emergency workers to their condition.

PEANUT ALLERGY

Of the various food allergies, an allergy to peanuts may be the most infamous. A measurable rise in the number of children with a peanut allergy and media interest in several long-term studies have increased awareness about this particular food allergy. Several studies have shown that the incidence of this allergy is rising. In 1989 on the Isle of Wight, in England, a study tracked children from birth until the age of four. It was found that 1.1 percent of them were allergic to peanuts by the age of four. A follow-up study in the mid-1990s showed that the number of children with the allergy had tripled. Other studies have demonstrated a similar increase.

Peanuts are a common ingredient in processed foods of various kinds. They are a cheap and plentiful source of protein, and they are useful as a thickener in sauces and soups. Many people with a mild peanut allergy do not suffer serious consequences if they eat peanuts. For people with a severe peanut allergy, however, even eating a food that has been manufactured near products containing peanuts can trigger an allergic reaction. In very rare cases, someone can have a reaction from breathing near someone else who has eaten the food. People with severe peanut allergies are quite restricted in the foods they can eat safely, and they must carefully read all food-product

oxide, pyridoxine hydrochloride (vitamin B₆ ...vin (vitamin B₂), thiamin hydrochloride (vit ...folic acid and vitamin B₁₂. To maintain qu ...has been added to the packaging.

CONTAINS WHEAT INGREDIENTS.

...ange: 3 Carbohydrates ...dietary exchanges are based on the *Exchange ...Meal Planning,* ©2003 by The American Dial ...ociation, Inc. and The American Dietetic Associa

In 2006, the Food and Drug Administration began requiring food manufacturers to list the presence of major allergens, including tree nuts, peanuts, milk, eggs, soybeans, and wheat, on all product labels.

ingredient labels and avoid certain cuisines. There are now recipes and special food products designed for people who cannot eat peanuts or other foods.

DIAGNOSIS AND TREATMENT OF FOOD ALLERGIES

In the case of moderate to severe allergies to foods such as shellfish or peanuts, the cause of the allergic reaction is usually already obvious. However, food allergies are often confirmed by skin-prick testing or radioallergosorbent (RAST) blood testing. These tests can be used to identify allergies to all kinds of substances, not just food.

Skin-prick testing is a virtually painless procedure, usually performed on a person's forearm. First the arm is cleaned, and then a liquid drop of allergen extract, containing minute amounts of the substance that may cause a reaction, is placed on the skin. A fine needle, or lancet, is used to prick through the droplet and into the skin. Usually a number of allergens are tested at the same time, at different places on the forearm. If the skin contains IgE antibodies for the substance being tested, there will be a swelling around the pinprick within around 15 minutes. The degree of swelling is also measured to determine how bad the allergy is. This test is inexpensive and reliable, and it can be used successfully on children and babies.

A RAST test is a blood test that examines the blood to see if it contains antibodies that will create different allergic reactions. This test is used mainly when a skin test would be unreliable; for example, if someone has a skin condition such as eczema or is taking medications such as antihistamines or antidepressants, then a RAST test would be indicated.

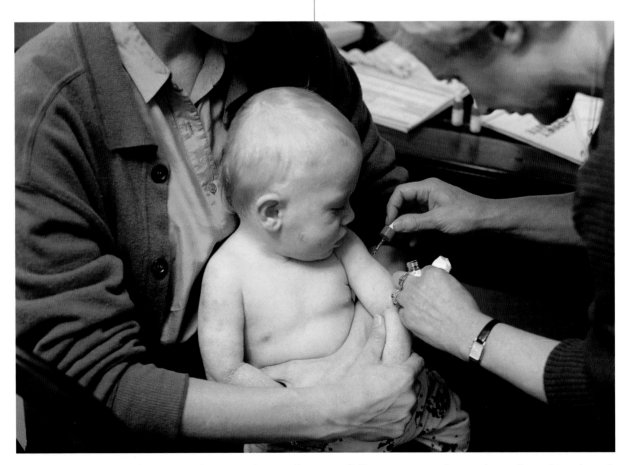

Skin-prick tests are a painless way to determine the specific cause of allergic reactions; they can be performed in a doctor's office on even the youngest of patients.

THE CAUSES OF FOOD ALLERGY: SOLUTIONS AND RESEARCH

Researchers are still trying to pinpoint exactly why allergies occur and how to prevent them. Many people with food allergies, and children in particular, have a history of asthma, and nearly all of them also have eczema. Scientists believe that fully understanding these connections may point them toward a cure for allergies. Research into the causes of peanut allergy has found definite connections between childhood eczema, asthma, and a propensity to develop the allergy. For instance, a research project entitled "Children of the 90s," which studied about 14,000 children in southwestern England, found links between the peanut allergy and both the consumption of soy milk and the use of peanut-oil skin creams and lotions. Babies did not appear to be born with the allergy; nor were they affected by whether their mother had eaten peanuts during pregnancy. However, research is still ongoing, and as with other food allergies, much is still unknown.

Advocacy groups have successfully lobbied for more information on labels about allergenic ingredients in food. The U.S. Food Allergen Labeling and Consumer Protection Act of 2004 (which applies to food products labeled on or after January 1, 2006) states that allergens in a food product must be listed on the packaging in clearly understandable language. Various groups have also asked for higher levels of funding for research into the causes and treatment of food allergies, as well as more accurate methods of detecting allergenic food ingredients. These are all valuable preventive measures.

In general, the best way to prevent a known allergic reaction is simply to avoid the food that causes it. This can be difficult when the food may be a hidden or minor ingredient in other food products (this is especially true for nuts and peanuts). Some people worry that the increase in genetically modified crops may be increasing the numbers of allergens in foods; others are considering whether crops can be genetically modified so that they will not cause allergies.

FURTHER READING

Books and articles

Brostoff, Jonathan. *The Complete Guide to Food Allergy and Intolerance*. London: Bloomsbury, 1998.

Frazier, Claude Albee. *Coping with Food Allergy*. New York: Quadrangle/New York Times Books, 1974.

National Institutes of Health Clinical Center. *Food Allergy and Intolerances*. Betheseda, MD: National Institutes of Health, 1993.

Sicherer, Scott H., and Terry Malloy. *The Complete Peanut Allergy Handbook*. New York: Berkley Books, 2005.

Walsh, William E. *Food Allergies: The Complete Guide to Understanding and Relieving Your Food Allergies*. New York: Wiley, 2000.

Willingham, Theresa. *Food Allergy Field Guide: A Lifestyle Manual for Families*. Littleton, CO: Savory Palate, 2000.

Web sites

The Food Allergy and Anaphylaxis Network.
Information on a variety of food allergies, with tips and recipes.
http://www.foodallergy.org

International Food Information Council (IFIC) Foundation: Understanding Food Allergy.
Information about food allergies and detailed information on foods and labeling. Also available in Spanish.
http://www.ific.org/publications/brochures/allergybroch.cfm

Medline Plus: Food Allergy.
Links to current information on food allergies, as well as general medical advice and information, from the U.S. National Institutes of Health.
http://www.nlm.nih.gov/medlineplus/foodallergy.html

SEE ALSO

Immune System; Intolerances; Labeling; Peanuts.

Aquaculture

Aquaculture is the practice of farming marine life, such as fish, shellfish, and even edible seaweed. Aquaculture has long been practiced in Asia, and it is becoming increasingly popular in the United States.

HOW AQUACULTURE WORKS

Many different kinds of aquatic life can be cultivated. In the United States, popular farmed fish include catfish, trout, salmon, bass, and tilapia for food, as well as smaller fish that are raised to be used as bait or for aquariums. The methods used for aquaculture vary, depending on the breed of fish. In most cases, fish farmers specialize in growing fish in one life

AQUACULTURE NUMBERS

In the early twenty-first century, roughly half the seafood eaten by people around the world was produced by aquaculture. The United States had roughly 4,000 fish farms as of 2005. Although this is a dramatic increase over the previous 20 years, it represents only 1 to 2 percent of aquaculture worldwide. China produces about 70 percent of the world's aquaculture.

stage. For example, certain farms, called hatcheries, focus on raising fish from eggs until they become juveniles. The young fish are then sold to conventional fish farmers, who continue to raise the fish until they are big enough to eat.

Hatcheries are nearly always built on land to create a tightly controlled environment that will ensure that the tiny hatchlings survive and grow. Conventional fish farms, however, can be built on land or in a body of water, such as a lake or the ocean. In such operations, fish are kept in underwater cages. Some fish, such as trout, need fast-moving streams and will not thrive in a stagnant pond or tank. These kinds of fish are raised in what are called raceways, which are a

Salmon pens at Port Esperance fish farm in Australia in 2003.

series of long, narrow, connected tanks. Water flows quickly from one tank to another, mimicking the action of a stream.

A ROYAL HISTORY

According to legend, fish farming was invented by Wen Wang, the founder of the Chou dynasty in China. In the twelfth century BCE, Wen Wang was confined to an estate by the last emperor of the Shang dynasty. During his imprisonment, Wen Wang built a pond and stocked it with fish. Although his methods were not recorded, the ancient text *Fish Culture Classic,* which was written about 460 BCE by a Chinese official named Fang Li, discusses how to build and stock a carp pond.

In Europe, oysters were being cultivated by the Romans by the first century CE, and carp and trout farming became common during the Middle Ages. The United States began to develop significant aquaculture operations during the nineteenth century, when trout were raised to be released into rivers and lakes.

A SOLUTION OR A PROBLEM?

The demand for fish has continued to grow, and aquaculture has been touted as a solution that provides necessary food while protecting wild fish. As currently practiced, however, aquaculture is plagued by controversy.

Many of the fish raised in farms are carnivores, and they are fed smaller fish as food. Those smaller fish are typically taken from the wild, suggesting that aquaculture will not lead to a reduction in fishing. In addition, these feeding practices may result in fish that are unsafe to eat. Studies of farmed salmon, for example, have found that they have higher concentrations of pollution in their bodies than wild salmon. Meanwhile, environmentalists have several concerns. Fish raised in ocean cages, as salmon often are, can escape and interbreed with wild fish, potentially weakening the genetic stock of the wild fish. In addition, when large numbers of farmed fish are crowded together into cages, their waste can seriously pollute the water around them. Diseases can also spread from the farmed fish to wild fish swimming past. Considerable research is under way to develop more environmentally friendly methods of aquaculture.

FURTHER READING

Books and articles

Lucas, John S., and Paul C. Southgate, eds. *Aquaculture: Farming Aquatic Animals and Plants.* Oxford, UK: Fishing News, 2003.

Parker, Rick. *Aquaculture Science.* Albany, NY: Delmar, 2002.

Web sites

SeaWeb: Aquaculture Resources.

Information on issues related to aquaculture.
http://www.seaweb.org/resources/
aquaculturecenter/index.php

U.S. National Oceanic and Atmospheric Administration: Aquaculture.

Data and information from NOAA on aquaculture.
http://www.nmfs.noaa.gov/aquaculture

SEE ALSO

Farming, Industrial; Fish.

Bacteria

Microscopic organisms known as bacteria are found living almost everywhere, including the inside of the human body. Some of the oldest fossils, from around 3.5 billion years ago, are of bacteria-like organisms. Many people associate bacteria with germs and infection, but they can also be beneficial. Research into bacteria is a relatively new field, and scientists think they may have discovered only around 5 percent of the hundreds of thousands of bacteria types in existence. Of these, only around two hundred kinds are pathogenic—that is, capable of causing diseases in humans.

Most food products contain bacteria. In some cases, bacteria are purposefully introduced into foods (such as yogurts and cheeses) as part of the manufacturing process.

BACTERIA AND FOOD-BORNE ILLNESS

Bacteria that are harmful to humans can grow on or in foods that are not stored or cooked properly.

- *Staphylococcus aureus* produces a protein in the human intestine that causes illness.
- *Clostridium botulinum* is found, rarely, in some meat products and other foods. *Escherichia coli* (E. coli) occurs in four strains that cause gastroenteritis in humans. Although the illness usually does not last long, it can be severe.
- *Salmonella* is found in eggs, poultry, and meats, and it can infect humans through contaminated raw foods or kitchen surfaces.

These, and many other kinds of bacteria that live inside the human body, are regarded as benign.

In its raw state, food that contains potentially harmful bacteria or has been in contact with other sources of bacteria can be dangerous to humans. Washing can remove unwanted bacteria from the surface of some foods. In other cases, cooking or heat treatments like pasteurization are necessary to destroy harmful bacteria that may contaminate foods such as meat and dairy products. Freezing and refrigeration can slow the growth of bacteria, but they do not stop bacteria growth completely.

WHAT ARE BACTERIA?

A single bacterium consists of one cell enclosed in a flexible outer membrane and, usually,

Two of the Most Common Types of Bacterial Cells

Bacilli

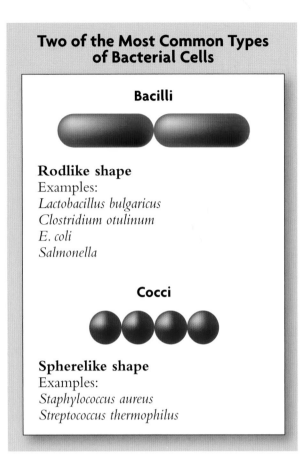

Rodlike shape
Examples:
Lactobacillus bulgaricus
Clostridium otulinum
E. coli
Salmonella

Cocci

Spherelike shape
Examples:
Staphylococcus aureus
Streptococcus thermophilus

BACTERIA IN THE HUMAN BODY

Nearly all animals and plants contain bacteria that live within them in a symbiotic (mutually beneficial) relationship. People and animals are born without any bacteria in their bodies, but they acquire bacteria soon after birth. The human body contains a huge number of beneficial bacteria, many of which live in the small and large intestines, where they play an essential role in the digestive process. These "friendly" bacteria form colonies in the large intestine, or colon, where they are known as microflora. Without these bacteria, a person would be weak and prone to infection from other bacteria. This is often temporarily the case in people who have had strong antibiotic treatments for bacterial illnesses, such as tuberculosis (TB), or for bacterial infections that result from other diseases, such as AIDS.

The bacteria in the large intestine digest carbohydrates, fats, and proteins, breaking them down into forms that can pass through the walls of the intestines and into the body as usable energy. As part of this digestive process, beneficial bacteria in the intestine synthesize several vitamins, such as biotin and pantothenic acid, which are B-complex vitamins that help in the release of energy from carbohydrates and proteins. Although

a rigid cell wall. Inside, a single DNA molecule floats within a substance called cytoplasm. This detail is impossible to see with the human eye, since bacteria are between 1 and 10 microns in diameter (1 micron equals a millionth of a meter, or approximately 1/25,000 inch). The first person to see and describe bacteria was Antoni van Leeuwenhoek (1632–1723), a Dutch cloth dealer, lens grinder, and amateur naturalist; he invented a microscope that was strong enough to reveal the small "animalcules," as he called them.

Bacteria are microorganisms that reproduce asexually, by cell division. Given the right conditions, bacteria can multiply at a very fast rate. However, in order to grow they need some kind of nutrition and a suitable temperature. Although many bacteria are heat-loving and multiply best at or above room temperature, there are some bacteria that can multiply in extremely cold conditions. Each type of bacteria is different, and bacteria come in all shapes and a range of sizes.

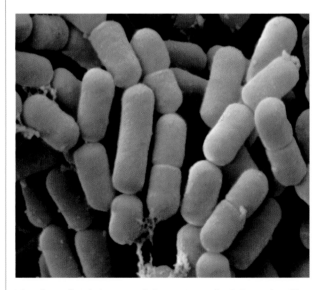

The beneficial intestinal bacteria called *Lactobacillus fermentum,* photographed through an electron microscope.

these vitamins are also present in foods, the bacteria ensure that the body receives sufficient quantities.

BACTERIA AND FOOD SAFETY

Many raw foods need to be cooked, washed, or treated in some other way to remove undesirable bacteria before they are eaten. Salad ingredients and other vegetables may have bacteria on them, for example, and raw meat, such as steak or chicken, may be covered with bacteria. Foods can also be contaminated by toxins, or poisonous substances, that are produced by the bacteria, and these toxins are often the cause of food poisoning. Bacteria may be introduced during harvesting or slaughter, or they may be present in the soil in which vegetables and fruits grow. However, the presence of bacteria does not necessarily mean that foods themselves are spoiled or unfit for human consumption.

Bacteria grow quickly in meat and foods with a high moisture content, such as fruit. If bacteria grow considerably, the food will change in composition and spoil; sometimes it will look moldy and taste bad. Eating such food may cause food poisoning, which can be serious (see box, Bacteria and Food-borne Illness). Refrigeration slows the growth but does not stop it completely. The bacteria in raw meat are killed by cooking, as long as the temperature is sufficiently high—normally at least 160°F (70°C). Ground meat must always be cooked very thoroughly, because any bacteria that were on the surface of the original meat will have been mixed into the meat as it was ground. Bacteria can also be transferred from raw meat to cooked meat by handling, and this is a common cause of food-borne illness.

Salad vegetables can be washed to remove dirt that may contain bacteria. However, if the water itself is unclean and contains bacteria, the food

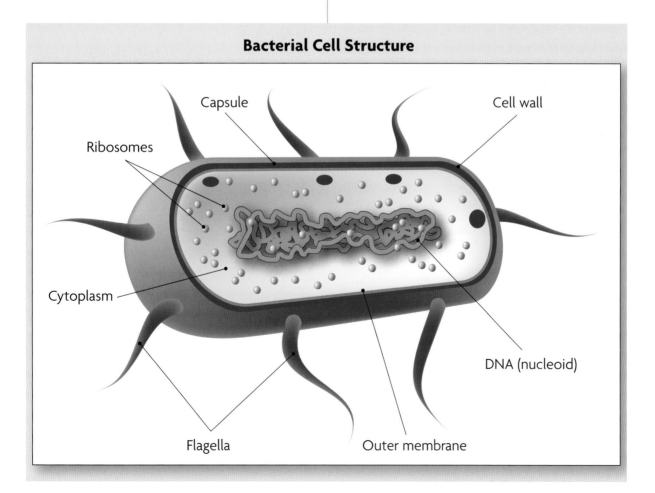

Bacterial Cell Structure

Capsule

Cell wall

Ribosomes

Cytoplasm

DNA (nucleoid)

Flagella

Outer membrane

can become contaminated by washing. This is a particular issue with vegetables that will be eaten raw. In areas without a reliable water supply, it is always important to be aware of this, for water contaminated by bacteria may not necessarily look dirty or taste bad. Since some bacteria grow quickly at temperatures between 40°F and 160°F (4°C and 70°C), it is also important not to leave prepared food out for more than an hour or two (as people sometimes do at parties).

Some forms of unwanted bacteria in food can be eliminated during processing. The heat treatment involved in canning fruits and vegetables kills all microorganisms present in the food. Food needs to be exposed to high temperatures for only a few seconds to achieve this, and it will retain most of its flavor and texture. Sugar also helps to slow bacterial growth when heated, as in the case of fruit jam (also known as fruit preserve). In some foods, such as fermented pickles and sauerkraut, bacteria themselves can help to preserve the food by killing other less beneficial bacteria. Another method used to destroy bacteria in meats is irradiation, a technique that uses radiation to destroy or reduce microorganisms in food.

DESIRABLE BACTERIA IN THE DIET

Bacteria are vital in the production of some foods, either as an essential ingredient or as a part of ingredient preparation. Yogurt is made by adding two specific beneficial bacteria, *Lactobacillus bulgaricus* and *Streptococcus thermophilus*, to sterilized milk. The bacteria feed on the sugars in the milk and curdle it, creating the distinctive taste and texture of yogurt. These live bacterial cultures (bacteria in a growing medium) can either be killed by heat treatment or left in the yogurt. These particular bacteria are welcome in the diet because they encourage the growth of beneficial resident bacteria in the human body and help to improve digestion. For this reason they are called probiotics.

Sourdough bread contains a strain of *Lactobacillus*. The bacteria feed on sugars and turn them into lactic acid. In breads made from conventional bakers' yeast, such an acidic environment would

prevent the dough from rising. However, sourdough is made using wild yeast, grown in a culture of flour and water, which thrives on lactic acid. This combination of bacteria and wild yeast gives the bread a distinctive sour flavor, as well as a good texture.

Bacteria are also used in the preparation of a surprising range of ingredients. In chocolate and coffee production, bacteria are used to eat the hard outer coating of the beans and make them ready for processing. Bacteria can also be used to make vinegar (from the French *vinaigre*, meaning "sour wine"). Particular strains of bacteria give different varieties of cheese a characteristic smell or rind. These strains are so important to the authenticity of the cheese that they are often closely guarded secrets.

FURTHER READING

Books

Albrecht, Julie A. *Microbes in Foods: The Good, the Bad, and the Ugly*. Lincoln, NE: Cooperative Extension, University of Nebraska, 1996.

Bailey, Jill. *Life in the Human Body*. Chicago: Raintree, 2004.

Favor, Lesli J. *Bacteria*. New York: Rosen, 2004.

Web sites

Great Scopes: Observing Bacteria Cultures in Yogurt. Information on how to grow bacteria.
   http://www.greatscopes.com/act010.htm

United States Department of Agriculture: Food Safety: Bacteria, Spoilage.

Information about bacteria and food-borne illness.
   http://www.fsis.usda.gov/help/FAQs_Food_Spoilage/index.asp

SEE ALSO

Canning; Digestion; Enzymes; Food-borne Illness; Irradiation; Refrigeration; Yogurt.

Baking

Baking is a way of cooking food in an oven using dry heat. In modern ovens, the heat is generated by an electric cooking element or gas flame. Since baking is a cooking technique rather than a cuisine, there is no "typical" baked food. Many types of foods are made by baking, from breads and pastries to soufflés and casseroles. Baking is the primary method used to cook breads, pies, cookies, and other pastries, and these foods are often called "baked goods."

BAKING IN HISTORY

Ovens were used by the Egyptians as early as the third century BCE to make flatbreads that would have been very similar to the Mexican tortilla or Indian chapati. Before gas and electric heat became common, baking ovens were heated by wood or coal fires. Keeping this type of oven at a high, consistent temperature for a long period of time required a great deal of work. In many towns and villages, bread was baked in communal ovens, which might be shared by all the families living in a particular area.

In the Middle Ages in most of western Europe, the person in charge of the public ovens came to be known as the baker (or the equivalent in other languages). Eventually, bakers also began to make and sell their own bread. However, bakers were notorious for their tendency to cheat, either by

TRY THIS...

Mix a teaspoon of fresh baking powder in a cup of hot water; there will be an immediate reaction. The bubbles produced are the result of the acidic ingredient in the baking powder (often cream of tartar) reacting with the water to produce carbon dioxide bubbles.

Bread being baked in a traditional, wood-fired brick oven. Baking in such ovens takes a lot of work to maintain a consistent temperature over time.

stealing dough from customers who brought their own, or by adding ingredients such as chalk to bread to make it look better. By 1266 the problem was so widespread in England, especially in London, that a law was passed (the Assize of Bread and Ale) that levied a fine on those bakers who cheated their customers.

Over the centuries, bakers continued to be essential shopkeepers, although many people in smaller communities did their baking at home. Since baking was, until modern times, an expensive cooking method in terms of fuel and equipment, people traditionally had a weekly "baking day" on which they made all their bread and other baked goods for the week.

Commercial bakeries began producing baked goods, especially bread, on a large scale in the nineteenth century. Modern, industrialized baking is largely automated, with machines doing nearly all the work. In the late twentieth century, mass-produced bread came to be criticized, particularly because of its added sugar and preservatives, which are designed to give bread a longer shelf life. Small, specialty bakeries, sometimes called artisanal bakeries, have become increasingly popular in the twenty-first century. They bake bread daily, using high-quality and often organic ingredients, and generally without using preservatives or added coloring.

HOW BAKING WORKS

Baking requires a consistent heat distributed throughout the oven to cook the food evenly. A specialized type of oven called a convection oven includes a fan that keeps the hot air moving continuously across the food, making it possible to bake at a lower overall temperature and for a shorter time than in a conventional oven.

Ingredients commonly used in baked products are flour, eggs, sugar, and some kind of fat. The quantities of each ingredient are very

A baker prepares *tunnbröd*, a Swedish flatbread, in the traditional way at a museum in Stockholm.

important and vary depending on the recipe. Because baking can involve a relatively long period of cooking, ingredients undergo significant changes during the process. For instance, the heat causes changes in the starches in flour; these changes make the surface of a cake or loaf turn brown.

To achieve a lighter, softer texture, air can be introduced into the recipe in a number of ways, including blending techniques that are used before the mixture goes into the oven, or through the use of raising agents such as yeast. These two methods are often used in combination. To introduce air, recipes for sweet baked goods start with a blending technique called creaming, which involves combining a fat, such as butter, with sugar until they form a light and fluffy mixture. Air is also introduced by beating eggs before mixing them with the dry ingredients. The eggs also act as an emulsifier; that is, they help other ingredients that do not mix well together (milk and oil, for instance) to be added, without curdling the mixture.

Air can also be added by the use of a rising or leavening agent, such as baking powder, baking soda (also called sodium bicarbonate), or yeast. The word *leaven* comes from the Latin *levare*, meaning "to raise," and refers to the fact that the mixture will rise up in the pan during the baking process. A rising agent produces a chemical reaction that creates carbon dioxide bubbles. These bubbles remain as open spaces after the liquid that formed them evaporates, creating a lighter texture.

BAKING AND NUTRITION

Traditional baking recipes often call for some type of fat to add both flavor and texture. Some cake and muffin recipes call for a white, colorless fat called shortening. Usually, shortening is a vegetable fat, although animal fat can also be used. Wheat-based doughs contain strands of gluten, a sticky protein that gives dough its elasticity and helps it to rise. The fat tenderizes the dough by reacting with the gluten and "shortening" the strands, creating a lighter baked good.

Many factory-produced baked goods contain trans fats. These fats are partially hydrogenated, using a process that changes their composition so that they are less likely to go rancid over time. Baked goods made from trans fats have a longer shelf life. However, trans fats also pose a health

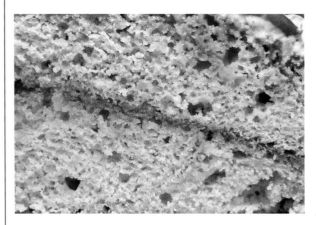

The airy texture of this cake is created by carbon dioxide bubbles.

HOW RISING AGENTS WORK

In general, most recipes for baked sweet foods use baking soda or powder to raise the food, whereas savory breads use yeast. Baking powder reacts when it gets hot and wet. Baking soda gradually reacts with the more acidic liquid ingredients of a recipe, such as buttermilk, milk, or yogurt. The many small bubbles produced can easily be seen in the texture of the baked food. They can be seen by looking at the cut surface of a slice of cake, for example.

Yeast is a "live" ingredient that feeds on sugars in ingredients, such as the starch in flour. In baking, yeast is usually first mixed with a small amount of liquid, such as milk, and often with a few teaspoons of sugar. Once it is activated it starts to grow, producing both carbon dioxide and alcohol (ethanol). In making yeast-raised bread the raw dough is left to "rise" for a period (sometimes two or more times) as the process of fermentation continues. During baking the alcohol evaporates, but the carbon dioxide that is created forms bubbles that give the dough its distinctive texture.

risk. Trans fats are known to raise the level of LDL ("bad") cholesterol in the blood and can lead to heart disease. Food labeling legislation in the United States requires manufacturers to state how much trans fat is in their packaged goods, although this is not the case for some fresh-baked goods and fast foods. Some baked goods also contain significant amounts of sugar.

Low-fat baking provides an alternative method for those who wish to reduce the amount of fat they eat, or to use only the fats that are considered more healthful. Although butter and eggs are mainstays of familiar baking recipes, they can often be successfully replaced by healthier, and sometimes surprising, substitutes, such as mashed bananas, raisin pastes, applesauce, or low-fat buttermilk.

FURTHER READING

Books and articles

Figoni, Paula. *How Baking Works: Exploring the Fundamentals of Baking Science.* New York: Wiley, 2003.

Johnson Dodge, Abigail, and Chuck Williams, eds. *Kids Baking.* San Francisco: Williams-Sonoma, 2003.

Web sites

Busy Cooks—Baking Ingredient Science.
Information on the roles of different ingredients in baking.
http://busycooks.about.com/library/archive/blingredrole.htm

Joy of Baking.
Site provides baking recipes for many occasions, a history of baking, and a further reading list.
http://www.joyofbaking.com

Science Explorer: Bubble bomb.
Experiments with baking soda that can be done at home.
www.exploratorium.edu/science_explorer/bubblebomb.html

SEE ALSO

Bread; Butter; Cooking Oils and Fats; Eggs; Trans Fats; Wheat; Whole Grains.

Barbecue

Barbecue (sometimes misspelled "barbeque" and thus shortened as BBQ) refers to a type of cooking that uses heat from smoking wood or charcoal to cook food. Because of the smoke, this type of cooking usually occurs outdoors. The term *barbecue* may be used as a verb to indicate the process of cooking in this fashion, or as a noun to refer either to the resulting food or to a gathering at which the food is served. The word can also be used to indicate a flavoring that is added to various foods, such as barbecue potato chips.

MURKY ORIGINS

As most people understand the term, barbecue is as old as cooking itself. The first instance of cooking undoubtedly occurred when our ancient ancestors had learned to create or harness fire and used it to char the meat of animals they hunted. In modern times, many people equate barbecuing with cooking food (usually meat or vegetables) over an open fire in some type of pit. This type of cooking has been practiced by every society around the world, from the time of earliest human activity to the present.

Barbecuing should be distinguished from grilling. Although the two terms are often used interchangeably, grilling simply means cooking food over a fire. Barbecuing, properly speaking, means cooking food slowly at a relatively low temperature, sometimes indirectly, using wood or charcoal as a heat source.

SAFE MINIMUM INTERNAL TEMPERATURES

- Whole poultry: 165°F (74°C)
- Poultry breasts: 165°F (74°C)
- Ground poultry: 165°F (74°C)
- Hamburgers, beef: 160°F (70°C)
- Beef, veal, and lamb (steaks, roasts, and chops):
  Medium rare 145°F (63°C)
  Medium 160°F (70°C)
- Pork (all cuts): 160°F (70°C)

Source: Food Safety Inspection Service, USDA.

Although over the years barbecue has come to most commonly refer to the cooking of pork, many other foods can be prepared in the same manner. Here, large pieces of salmon are cooked slowly over an open, wood-burning fire pit in British Columbia, Canada.

The history of barbecuing is uncertain, but food historians believe that the cooking method has its origin in the Caribbean. From there it spread to the American South, where barbecue—especially barbecued pork—has become a cultural and culinary fixture. Early Spanish explorers brought swine with them from Europe. These animals, introduced into the wilds of what is now Florida, quickly reproduced and spread along the Atlantic and Gulf coasts. Unlike the meat of domesticated hogs, the meat of these semi-wild pigs was tough and not particularly savory. Settlers found that long, slow cooking over a wood fire rendered it much more appetizing. Although the science was probably unknown at the time, modern nutritionists understand that this slower method of cooking breaks down the connective tissue called collagen in meat, tenderizing it considerably.

A SOUTHERN CULTURAL INHERITANCE

Although barbecue is associated with other regions in the United States, and although other countries (Korea and Mongolia, to name two of the best known) have their own barbecue traditions, nowhere has barbecue been more thoroughly developed and cherished than in the American South. After its introduction, barbecue became central to the lives of poor southerners, who continued to rely on the plentiful semi-wild pigs for food. The hunt for these pigs was often a group affair and occasioned celebrations after the slaughter was done. The association of barbecue with large gatherings of people arose from these early days.

Pork was clearly the staple meat of the southern diet: prior to the Civil War, southerners ate five times more pork than beef. Slow cooking over an open fire—often in a pit requiring the ministrations of experienced "pitmen," who tended the fire and ensured that the meat was properly smoked—was the preferred way to prepare pork.

The "pitmen," or "pit masters," as they are sometimes called, have been central to the traditional southern barbecue. The day before a barbecue was scheduled, these men would dig a pit in the ground and fill it with hardwood. This wood was then burned down to coals. Whole pigs were suspended over the pit by skewers while the pitmen would tend them all through the night, regulating the coals and turning the spits. The next day, the meat was pulled off the carcass and finished with the preferred sauce of the region. A traditional barbecue, therefore, is often referred to as "a pig pickin.'" In the twenty-first century, political rallies and church gatherings in the South are still coupled with an old-fashioned barbecue, and barbecue restaurants (often called "joints") are everywhere.

There are many regional variations of barbecue across the South. In North Carolina, pork that has been slow-cooked and then pulled apart by hand is served with a tangy vinegar sauce and eaten as a sandwich. In South Carolina, the pork is prepared in the same manner but is finished with a mustard-based sauce, whereas in Memphis, Tennessee, a sweet, tomato-based sauce is more typical. (Memphis hosts the annual "Memphis in May" World Championship Barbecue Cooking Contest, which draws some 100,000 barbecue lovers from around the world.)

In Texas and Oklahoma, pork typically gives way to beef (especially brisket) as the meat of choice. Still, the principle of long, slow cooking over an open fire applies. The type of wood used

COOKING WITH DRY HEAT

Barbecuing is just one of several types of cooking using dry heat, usually from a wood or charcoal fire (rather than steam or boiling water). Here are several terms for different ways of dry-cooking food:

- Cold smoking (used for ham and salmon). The meat is first cured using salt, sugar, and nitrates. It is then smoked for a long period at 90°F (32°C). The meat is preserved but not dried, and it absorbs the smoke flavor.

- Hot smoking. This technique is similar to barbecuing, and many consider the two to be the same. Other experts differentiate hot smoking as occurring at temperatures up to 190°F (88°C), used for such foods as sausage. This method takes several hours, and it partially cooks and flavors the meat with smoke but does not preserve it.

- Barbecuing. This is often regarded as occurring at approximately the boiling point of water (212°F or 100°C) and can take from a few hours to up to a day (depending on the meat). Barbecuing fully cooks the meat and imparts a smoke flavor to it, but it does not preserve the meat.

- Roasting. This typically occurs at 350°F (180°C), although food can roast at temperatures between 250°F and 450°F (120°C and 235°C). Roasting cooks the meat completely and relatively quickly but gives it little smoke flavor.

- Broiling. This occurs at 500°F (260°C) or even much higher. Broiling fully cooks the meat quickly but typically gives it no smoke flavor.

in the cooking varies also, lending different flavors to the meat. Most popular are hickory, oak, apple, or wood from other fruit trees. In Texas, mesquite is often used.

BEYOND THE SOUTH

The barbecue method, as described here, is largely unique to the southern United States, but it has, of course, become popular beyond that region. Many people all over the world take pains to barbecue, and not simply grill, their meat. A wide range of other foods, such as fish, chicken, fruits, and vegetables, can be cooked over an open fire, but they are grilled relatively quickly, rather than enduring the slow-cook method of barbecue.

Outside the United States, most preparations calling themselves barbecue do not actually involve its distinctive long, slow-cook method. A favorite Korean dish, *bulgogi*, is thinly sliced beef that is marinated in a spicy soy sauce and then cooked over a grill—often at the diner's table in a Korean restaurant. While it is sometimes called "Korean BBQ," *bulgogi* actually means "fire beef," referring, no doubt, both to the meat's spiciness and to the way it is cooked.

Regions around the world have their own out-door food preparation traditions. In the Caribbean, where the barbecue method was, arguably, first

Caribbean-style jerk seasoning is a blend of allspice, Scotch bonnet peppers, scallions, nutmeg, and other ingredients. It is used to spice up pork, goat, fish, and chicken (above) before barbecuing.

observed, the style of jerked pork (in which the meat is dry-rubbed with a very hot spice mixture that includes Scotch bonnet peppers, then is wrapped in banana leaves and cooked in a pit over smoldering pimento wood) remains popular and is a form of cooking akin to barbecue. Like *barbecue*, the term *jerk* refers both to the cooking technique and to the food cooked by that method (as well as to the spice mixture).

FURTHER READING

Books and articles

Elie, Lolis Eric. *Smokestack Lightning: Adventures in the Heart of Barbecue Country*. Berkeley, CA: Ten Speed, 2005.

Hale, Smoky. *The Great American Barbecue and Grilling Manual*. McComb, MS: Abacus, 2000.

Huntley, Dan, and Lisa Grace Lednicer. *Extreme Barbecue: Smokin' Rigs and Real Good Recipes*. San Francisco: Chronicle, 2007.

Walsh, Robb. *Legends of Texas Barbecue*. San Francisco: Chronicle, 2002.

Web sites

BBQ: A Southern Cultural Icon.

Brief history of barbecue by Laura Dove, with an especially good discussion of its role in Southern culture.

http://xroads.virginia.edu/~class/MA95/dove/bbq.html

SEE ALSO

Caribbean Cuisine; Grilling; Korean Cuisine; Pork; Smoked Foods.

Beef

Beef cattle have played a role in human history since prehistoric times, and they are still considered a form of wealth in many cultures. Beef has long been the most popular meat in the United States. Like other meats, beef is a high-quality source of protein and it supplies many essential vitamins and minerals. However, beef is also high in cholesterol and saturated fats.

CHARACTERISTICS AND NUTRITION

Good-quality beef is firm, fine-grained tissue that is dark red in color because of the presence of myoglobin, a red protein that contains iron and

THE "DONENESS" OF BEEF

- Rare beef: internal temperature, 125°F to 130°F (52°C to 54°C); red center; gray–brown surface; soft and juicy meat.
- Medium-rare: internal temperature, 130°F to 140°F (54°C to 60°C); pink center; gray–brown surface.
- Medium: internal temperature, 140°F to 150°F (60°C to 66°C); slightly pink center becoming gray–brown toward surface.
- Medium well-done: internal temperature, 150°F to 160°F (66°C to 70°C); mostly gray center; firm texture.
- Well-done: internal temperature, 160°F (70°C); gray-brown throughout.

is found in the muscles of mammals and birds. Fat cells between the muscle fibers produce an effect that is known as marbling, which is considered desirable in meat because the fat adds tenderness. Veal, or meat from young calves, is pale pinkish gray in color, rather than red. This difference in color occurs because the calves are fed a special liquid diet that contains a limited amount of iron, and their bodies cannot produce much myoglobin.

Like other proteins from animal sources, beef is a "complete protein": it contains all of the nine essential amino acids that cannot be produced by the human body. Protein is the basic structural material of all cells, including those in the body's tissues, organs, and bones. Protein also makes up the hormones and enzymes, regulates all the body's processes, and works with the immune system to combat disease. In addition, protein can be used as an energy source. A three-ounce (85 g) serving of lean beef provides 50 percent of the recommended daily amount of protein.

Beef contains a number of important vitamins and minerals. Calorie for calorie, it is one of the best dietary sources of many essential B vitamins, including thiamine (vitamin B_1), riboflavin (B_2), and B_{12}. These vitamins help release the energy contained in food. Beef is also rich in iron, a mineral that helps carry oxygen to the body's cells and tissues. Iron helps produce new red blood cells, contributes to brain development, and supports the immune system. Like other red meats, such as lamb, beef does not just contain iron; it also improves the body's absorption of iron from plant sources. This effect is known as the "meat factor."

Zinc, another mineral supplied by beef, is important for proper growth and development, maintaining the immune system, healing wounds, and controlling appetite. A three-ounce (85 g) serving of beef provides 39 percent of the normal daily requirement for zinc. Other essential nutrients found in beef include the trace mineral selenium, an antioxidant that works with vitamin E to prevent cell damage; choline, a mineral that plays an important role in thinking and memory functions; and conjugated linoleic acid (CLA), a fatty acid that has been shown to stimulate the immune system. Other potential benefits from CLA are under study.

All of these nutritional benefits must be balanced against an important drawback: beef is relatively high in cholesterol and saturated fats, which can contribute to heart disease and other health problems if this meat is consumed in excess. Of course, some dietary fat is necessary. Fat provides for the absorption of fat-soluble vitamins, helps to

BEEF: NUTRITION INFORMATION

TYPE OF BEEF	SERVING SIZE	ENERGY (kcal)	PROTEIN (g)	TOTAL FAT (g)	SODIUM (mg)	CHOLESTEROL (mg)	RIBOFLAVIN (VITAMIN B$_2$) (mg)	IRON (mg)
Bottom round	3 oz. (85 g)	178	27	7	43	82	0.22	2.9
Corned beef	3 oz. (85 g)	213	23	13	855	73	0.12	1.8
Frankfurter	1 frank (45 g)	142	5	13	462	27	0.05	0.6
Ground beef	3 oz. (85 g)	246	20	18	71	77	0.16	2.1
Liver	3 oz. (85 g)	184	23	7	90	410	3.52	5.3
Roast, eye of round	3 oz. (85 g)	143	25	4	53	59	0.14	1.7
Roast, rib	3 oz. (85 g)	195	23	11	61	68	0.18	2.4
Steak, sirloin	3 oz. (85 g)	166	26	6	56	76	0.25	2.9

Notes: Bottom round (relatively lean, lean only, cooked); corned beef (canned); frankfurter (all beef); ground beef (73 percent lean, broiled); liver (slice, fried); roast, rib (relatively fat, lean only oven-cooked, no liquid added); roast, eye of round (relatively lean, lean only oven-cooked, no liquid added); steak, sirloin (lean only, broiled).

Source: U.S. Department of Agriculture, Agricultural Research Service, USDA Nutrient Data Laboratory. USDA National Nutrient Database for Standard Reference, Release 19. 2006. Available from http://www.ars.usda.gov/nutrientdata.

An 1895 advertisement from the St. Louis Beef Canning Company shows cowboys herding beef cattle in Missouri.

produce certain hormones, and can provide energy. However, many people in the Western world consume more fat than is necessary. To limit fat intake when consuming beef, it is advisable to select leaner cuts of meat and to limit portion size to around three ounces (85 g)—an amount roughly the size of a pack of playing cards.

HISTORY, GEOGRAPHY, AND CULTURE

Cattle were domesticated as long ago as 7000 BCE. They were raised for their milk, were made to perform work such as pulling plows, and provided a source of meat and leather. In its etymology, the word *cattle* is close to *chattel,* or personal property. A physical form of wealth, cattle were used as currency in some cultures.

Modern patterns of beef consumption reflect different culinary and religious traditions. Beef consumption and production in Great Britain and the European Union countries were once high, but they declined sharply in the wake of the epidemic of "mad cow disease," or bovine spongiform encephalopathy (BSE), in the 1980s and 1990s. Lamb, rather than beef, is the preferred meat in the Middle East. The wealthier classes in some African countries eat beef, but it is virtually nonexistent in the diets of the poorer classes. Cattle are revered by Hindus, and beef is forbidden under that religion's dietary laws. It is therefore not generally eaten in India or other nations or regions where Hinduism is the main religion. Many Buddhists, in Asia and elsewhere, choose to eat a vegetarian diet for religious reasons.

Workers wash carcasses at a slaughterhouse in Toluca, Mexico, in 2004.

Cattle raising played a significant role in shaping U.S. history. Among its more colorful aspects is the figure of the cowboy, who has been romanticized and celebrated in literature, song, and movies. The original cowboys were indigenous Mexicans, called *vaqueros* in Spanish. As early as the sixteenth century, *vaqueros* were enslaved by the Spanish and put to work tending herds under extremely harsh conditions. In the mid-1800s, cattle ranching boomed in the western United States in response to a mounting demand for beef in the North and East. Cattle were sometimes taken to market using the newly built western railroad. In other cases they went to the stockyards "on the hoof," in massive cattle drives. After the Civil War, many freed slaves traveled west to work on round-ups and cattle drives. Between 1866 and 1895, an estimated 8,000 African American cowboys (25 percent of the total number of cowboys) herded cattle up the trail from Texas.

By the mid-1800s, Chicago had emerged as a major center for the sale, slaughter, and packing of beef cattle and other livestock. By the turn of the twentieth century, Chicago's meatpacking industry was controlled by a few large companies (sometimes called the "beef trust"). A young investigative journalist, Upton Sinclair, documented the filthy conditions and misery of the workers at the packing-houses. Sinclair used his eyewitness account as the basis for his explosive novel *The Jungle,* published in 1906. An instant best seller, *The Jungle* generated

a huge public outcry and contributed to the passage of the Pure Food and Drug Act and the related Meat Inspection Act that same year.

BEEF FARMING AND PROCESSING

Modern beef production incorporates many scientific advances. By the end of the twentieth century, there were some 90 breeds of cattle raised specifically for beef, as compared with around 40 in the 1970s. As a result of consumer demand, modern beef cattle are bred to be as much as 27 percent leaner than they were in the late 1970s.

Beef cattle are usually fed some combination of pasture grasses and hay, straw, grain (corn, sorghum, wheat, barley, or oats), and supplements to provide them with protein and minerals. Cattle being fattened for slaughter are typically fed from 2.2 to 3 percent of their live weight daily, and they gain from 2 to 3 pounds (1.0 to 1.4 kg) each day. Up until the late 1970s, fattening cattle were given a synthetic hormone called diethylstilbestrol (DES), which produced a 10 to 20 percent increase in daily weight gain with less feed. The use of DES in cattle was outlawed in 1979, however, when it was linked to numerous health problems in humans.

Almost all beef in the United States comes from cattle that are younger than 20 months old at slaughter, because the meat at this age is more tender than that of older cattle. At the slaugh-

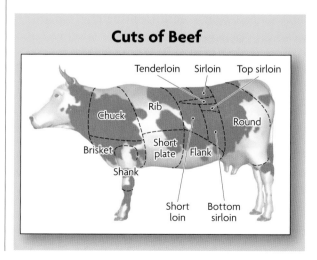

Cuts of Beef

Two breeds of beef cattle: two white Charolais, a breed that originated in central France and became globally important after World War II; and one red Angus, a breed that originated in Scotland in the mid-eighteenth century.

terhouse, the animals are stunned, or rendered unconscious, before being killed. The carcasses are then suspended upside down by a hind leg and bled. The heads and skin are removed, the carcass is split into "sides," and the internal organs are removed. The sides are hung to cool at a controlled rate. Government inspections to ensure proper hygiene occur at several stages throughout the slaughter and packing processes. A beef carcass is divided into primal (or major) cuts—the basic sections from which steaks, roasts, and briskets are carved, as well as smaller cuts of beef.

According to U.S. Department of Agriculture (USDA) guidelines, eight cuts of beef are classified as lean: eye round, top round, round tip, top sirloin, bottom round, top loin, tenderloin, and flank steak. In addition to the standard cuts of beef, some people like to eat what are called "variety meats," which include the tongue, liver, kidneys, brains, glands commonly known as "sweetbreads" (the pancreas and thyroid), and testicles (which are known by such names as "prairie oysters" and "Rocky Mountain oysters"). The blood of cattle is sometimes used as an ingredient in sausage.

Aging is a process that helps tenderize beef by giving the collagen, a protein tissue, time to relax. In the traditional, dry-aging method, an entire carcass or large cut is hung in a temperature-controlled cooler for three weeks or longer. The meat loses moisture, and a distinctive flavor develops. This method is becoming less usual, however, and tends to be used only with a small percentage of prime-grade beef, which is then sold at high prices. Most beef now undergoes a "wet-aging" process. In this method, the fresh cuts are vacuum-packed in plastic bags, a process called Cryovac, and allowed to rest at temperatures of 34°F to 38°F (1.1°C to 3.3°C) for one to four weeks. The beef does age and become more tender inside the plastic, but it retains all its moisture and does not acquire the same flavor that dry-aging produces.

GRADES OF BEEF AND SPECIAL LABELING

Since 1927, the USDA has operated a voluntary beef-grading system, and most processors pay to have government inspectors assign and stamp carcasses with a grade indicating quality. There are eight grades, but only the three highest— prime, choice, and select—are sold to consumers (the lower grades are used commercially for canned products, such as soups or stews). Only about 2 percent of beef is rated prime, and this meat tends to be sold to upscale restaurants and hotels. Of the two grades available in supermarkets, choice is more tender and has more fat, whereas select is leaner and is often sold in ground form.

In addition to the grade, consumers may see special labels on beef. A label such as Certified Hereford Beef or Certified Angus Beef indicates the breed of cattle the meat comes from. Grass-fed beef has been raised mostly on pasture forage rather than in a feedlot. Organic beef has been produced without hormones, pesticides, or other chemicals. Kosher beef is certified to have been butchered in accordance with Jewish dietary laws. Halal beef is certified to have been processed in accordance with Muslim dietary laws.

COOKING BEEF

The most suitable method for cooking beef depends largely on the cut. The more tender (and generally more expensive) cuts benefit from dry cooking methods (such as grilling, broiling, and roasting) that use relatively high temperatures and short cooking times. For tougher cuts from the chuck, brisket, and flank, a moist-heat cooking method, such as stewing or braising the meat in liquid at lower temperatures for longer times, works best.

The question of the "doneness" of cooked beef applies to grilled, broiled, or roasted cuts, and to ground beef. Standard terms have evolved to describe how thoroughly meat is cooked (see box, The Doneness of Beef). Because of the risk of bacterial contamination of meat—especially ground meat like hamburger—health experts generally recommend that meat be cooked thoroughly, but many people prefer to eat beef that is somewhat rare.

ENVIRONMENTAL IMPACT

Many environmentalists believe that as the world's population increases, the consumption of beef will severely strain resources or even become an unaffordable luxury. Beef is indeed costly in terms of land use—the same amount of grain used to fatten a single steer could feed many people. In addition, the wastewater that drains off from feedlots carries contaminants from the animals' body wastes and can pollute groundwater. Cattle also emit methane gas, which contributes from all its sources about 4 to 9 percent to global warming.

In Central and South America, cattle ranching is a main cause of rain forest destruction. Ranchers slash and burn the forests to grow pasture grass for their beef cattle, whose meat often ends up in fast-food hamburgers and as frozen meat in the United States. Loss of the rain forests means that dozens of plant and animal species lose their habitats. Both deforestation and overgrazing can lead to desertification, or the drying up of land into desert, which in turn sets the stage for dust-bowl conditions. In 2003 it was determined that a large cloud of dust in the western United States was the result of overgrazing and wind erosion in China.

FURTHER READING

Books and articles

Edge, John T. *Hamburgers and Fries.* New York: Putnam, 2005.

Lovenheim, Peter. *Portrait of a Burger as a Young Calf: The Story of One Man, Two Cows, and the Feeding of a Nation.* New York: Harmony, 2002.

Rifkin, Jeremy. *Beyond Beef: The Rise and Fall of the Cattle Culture.* New York: Plume, 1993.

Sinclair, Upton. *The Jungle.* 1906. New York: Penguin Classics, 2006.

Web sites

National Cattlemen's Association.

This site features information on the cattle industry and beef production.

http://www.beef.org

SEE ALSO

Amino Acids; Bovine Spongiform Encephalopathy; Cholesterol; Iron; Protein; Saturated Fats.

Beriberi

Beriberi is a vitamin-deficiency disease that causes muscle weakness and nerve damage. It occurs in people whose diet consists mainly of polished grains, such as white rice and white flour. The word *beriberi* means "I cannot" in Sinhalese, a language of Sri Lanka, and describes the extreme weakness that people experienced when they had beriberi.

HISTORY OF BERIBERI

In the late 1800s and early 1900s in Europe and Asia, polished white rice and white flour became more common in the food supply. To make white rice and white flour, the outer coating (bran) of the grain

FOODS WITH THIAMINE

- Whole grains and whole grain cereals

- White bread, pasta, rice (fortified with thiamine)

- Fortified breakfast cereals

- Lean pork

- Legumes (kidney beans, garbanzos, lentils, split peas, and others)

kernels is polished off. Scientists did not realize at the time that this process removes compounds important for good health (these compounds later turned out to be vitamins).

In a famous study, A. G. Vorderman (1844–1905), a physician in the Dutch civil service, posted in the Dutch East Indies (now Indonesia), discovered that prisoners in the Dutch East Indies who ate only polished white rice developed weak muscles, but prisoners who ate "red rice," which still had its bran coating, did not lose muscle strength. Unfortunately, the red rice was not very popular.

In 1925 the first B vitamin, called thiamine, was identified by Dutch scientists studying

Whole-grain products such as pasta and bread are rich in thiamine.

beriberi in Indonesia. Thiamine is the vitamin in the bran coating that prevents beriberi.

SYMPTOMS OF BERIBERI

Beriberi is actually two different illnesses: dry beriberi and wet beriberi. Dry beriberi affects the nervous system. People with dry beriberi are pale, thin, listless, and weak, and their arms and legs feel weak and tingly ("pins and needles"). They may also feel sore and have muscle cramps. People who abuse alcohol can develop a similar thiamine-deficiency disease called Wernicke-Korsakoff syndrome. The disease affects the brain; patients become confused and forgetful, have trouble with their balance, and may fall into a coma.

People with wet beriberi also are pale and malnourished, but wet beriberi affects the heart rather than the nervous system. People with wet beriberi have swollen arms and legs because their hearts cannot pump blood properly.

In the early stages of beriberi, people generally feel tired. They may be depressed and act crankier than usual, and concentration becomes difficult. Beriberi causes a loss of appetite, stomach pain, and even nausea and vomiting.

BERIBERI TODAY

Beriberi rarely occurs in the United States, where most processed grains are fortified with added thiamine and other vitamins and minerals. However, people who abuse alcohol over a long period of time may develop beriberi because alcohol prevents the body from using thiamine normally. The disease also still occurs in countries that do not add vitamins to their processed flours and grain foods. Beriberi remains common in Indonesia, where the incidence among low-income Indonesians is more than 60 percent.

The main treatment for beriberi is thiamine supplements. People with wet beriberi improve quickly after they are given thiamine. Dry beriberi is a more serious illness, however, and it takes longer to treat because the nervous system heals more slowly.

FURTHER READING

Books and articles
Carpenter, Kenneth. *Beriberi, White Rice, and Vitamin B: A Disease, a Cause, and a Cure.* Berkeley: University of California Press, 2000.

Web sites
MedlinePlus: Beriberi.
The U.S. National Library of Medicine and the National Institutes of Health have teamed up to provide a medical encyclopedia with links to additional information.
http://www.nlm.nih.gov/medlineplus/ency/article/000339.htm
WebMD: Beriberi.
A comprehensive overview of beriberi, written by a doctor.
www.emedicine.com/ped/topic229.htm

SEE ALSO

Grains; Whole Grains.

Body Image

The term *body image* refers to how people judge the shape and size of their bodies, as well as the feelings they have about their bodies. People who are satisfied with their appearance are said to have a positive body image, whereas people with a negative body image are unhappy about their bodies in some respect. Body image is personal and subjective, in that it relates to an individual's perception of his or her body rather than to any external opinion. Someone who has a negative body image may in fact seem perfectly normal in appearance to others, and indeed may be considered very attractive.

Most people with a negative body image are extremely self-critical and are unable to look at their bodies as a whole. Instead, they may focus on a part of the body that they feel is unpleasant or deficient. For example, a person may feel he or she has a big nose, and this one part of the body may become the focus of attention, to the exclusion of everything else. People with a negative body image also tend to view their bodies in isolation, as separate from their personality, intelligence, and other qualities.

A study conducted at the University of Arizona in 2000 found that 90 percent of teenage girls thought frequently about their body shape. Such concerns can lead to serious long-term health problems. For example, an obsession with body image is one of the symptoms of anorexia nervosa and bulimia. On the other hand, surveys have shown that many obese American men regard themselves as only slightly overweight and tend to have a positive body image.

BARBIE AND GI JOE

If Barbie were life-size:
- She would be 5 foot 9 inches (1.8 m) and weigh 110 pounds (50 kg), severely underweight for her height.
- She would be so top-heavy that she could probably not stand up for long.

If GI Joe Extreme were life-size:
- He would have a 55-inch (1.4-m) chest and 27-inch (0.7-m) biceps.
- His biceps would be as big as his waist.

Many factors influence the development of an irrational negative body image. Pressures from family and society, especially the media, may be a factor, and a genetic predisposition to anxiety and depression can also be a contributing factor. Throughout history, ideals of physical beauty have changed significantly, and many people have been conditioned to want a certain, usually unrealistic, body shape.

BODY IMAGE AND HEALTH

Body image is intertwined with self-esteem. Concerns about body image often begin around the time of puberty, when young people, especially young women, are experiencing changes in their bodies. At a time when being attractive may seem particularly important, perceived problems with body shape and size can cause many young people to feel anxious, and this anxiety can lead to depression. A young woman who dislikes the way her body looks may feel that everyone she meets is regarding her with disgust. If such a person already has low esteem for other reasons, or has additional mental health issues, a negative body image may develop. Such people can find it difficult to

THE "IDEAL" FEMALE BODY

Body image is strongly influenced by what is considered to be the fashionable body of the day. Throughout history the ideal body type has changed in response to pressures from society and the media. This trend is particularly true of women's body shapes.

- In the 1800s the ideal female body was one with a small waist and full hips and breasts. To achieve this appearance, women wore corsets that were extremely tight and caused breathing problems.
- In the early 1900s slimness became more fashionable. By the 1920s the trend was toward "boyish" figures in women, and women bound their breasts to achieve a flat look.
- In the 1950s a large bustline (breasts) and thin body became the fashion. Women were "curvy," as epitomized by voluptuous celebrities like Marilyn Monroe.
- The 1960s saw a move back toward boyish slimness, and this trend became even more prominent in the 1970s.
- By the 1980s the "ideal body" for women was slim and toned, with an athletic look. The 1990s saw a preference for very slim women with large (often surgically enhanced) breasts, an image that remained in vogue into the twenty-first century.

An advertisement for magnetic corsets, 1890. Various forms of corsets were used for centuries—usually by women but occasionally also by men—to mold the body into a "desirable" shape. An ill-fitting corset could cause damage to the rib cage, stomach, intestines, or liver.

Models on the runway at the opening of the Singapore Fashion Festival in 2007. Responding to concerns about eating disorders in the fashion world, organizers instituted a policy forbidding "unnaturally thin" models from participating in the show.

socialize, and they become withdrawn. For both men and women, and in particular for young adults, attempts to attain the ideal body may trigger eating or exercise disorders, as well as other health problems. Studies indicate that young women, in particular, may start smoking, or they may follow fad diets in an attempt to change their appearance.

When people are habitually negative about their bodies, it can be hard for them to change their attitudes and become more positive without outside help. Their feelings may be out of proportion with reality, and their mental distress may even become disabling. Since body image is primarily psychologically defined, rather than reflecting a physical reality, people may retain a negative body image no matter how much they do to change their shape and size.

In nurturing a positive body image, it is important to look for the positive in one's appearance, maintain a healthy body weight, and eat as balanced a diet as possible. These changes can be very hard to achieve if a person has ingrained feelings of negative body image, and help from a doctor, counselor, or dietician can be invaluable. However, many people with negative body image do not seek help.

BODY IMAGE AND THE MEDIA

In the contemporary world there is an intense and constant pressure to look a certain way and to have a certain kind of body shape. Even young children may be influenced by the shape of their dolls. In Western society the media play a large part in drawing attention to body image through movies, television shows, and magazines. Women are urged to be extremely slender, and men are told they need to have a toned, muscular, tall body in order to be considered attractive. Most main-stream media images of the body in Western

The cover of *Time* magazine depicts the 1937 Woman of the Year: American-born heiress, and Duchess of Windsor, Wallis Simpson. Simpson exemplified a twentieth century upper-class American obsession with slimness with the statement that "one can never be too thin or too rich."

STEPS TO A REALISTIC BODY IMAGE

Young people are bombarded with media images of impossibly beautiful men and women, with toned bodies and perfect features. The media feature far fewer images of "normal" people, and a person can easily come to believe that he or she needs to look like these celebrities to be happy and successful. There is also enormous peer pressure among young people to conform to the latest fashion or trend.

It is important to realize that media images are very unrealistic. The models and celebrities are not typical. Also, many of the images are changed by computers, making people look even thinner than they really are and hiding blemishes and imperfections. In a sense, most media images are completely imaginary, and they do not reflect real life.

People come in all shapes and sizes. Being of normal weight and following a healthy diet are the best ways not only to look good, but to feel good as well. In confronting media and society's pressures to conform to a particular body type, people need to remember that:

- Media representations of the body are unrealistic and are often fabricated.
- Not all bodies are the same, and not all people look the same.
- Weight gain and changes in body shape are normal during puberty.

culture present white North American or European bodies as the ideal, and the normal body shapes of other cultures are seldom represented.

For most people, the body shapes presented by the media are impossible to achieve, especially since many media images of the body are fabricated or enhanced. For instance, magazine photographs are routinely touched up or changed using computer software in order to make a model's figure or skin seem more ideal than it is. In addition, celebrities follow strict diet and exercise regimes that most people cannot afford or do not have time to achieve. However, such is the power of the media that many people—not only younger people—constantly compare their own bodies with these images. As a result, they become dissatisfied with their bodies and develop a negative body image.

Male Body Image

In the past, there was less pressure on men than on women to conform to a single stereotypical look. However, in contemporary Western society there is a glamour associated with males who have an athletic and muscular appearance. For example, the "ripped" or "cut" look of a toned male body, with visible muscles and very little extra fat, has become the fashion. A rise in the proportion of men diagnosed with eating disorders points toward a greater prevalence of negative body image in men, particularly in young men.

The increase in the number of men with a negative and distorted body image may be related to the media's presentation of male sports stars as role models, and to other factors such as childhood teasing and peer pressure to be tough. Like women, some men may also try to make radical changes to their body size by excessive exercise or dieting, which can lead to illness. Men may resort to steroid use to enhance muscle definition, with serious mental and physical side effects. Some surveys indicate that 50 percent of young men are dissatisfied with some aspect of their bodies.

BODY DYSMORPHIC DISORDER

Many people have a negative body image, but body dysmorphic disorder (BDD) is a recognized mental illness that is much more serious. Anorexia nervosa is a form of BDD, since people with this eating disorder will see themselves as overweight and unattractive, even if they are of average weight and appearance.

People with BDD are constantly worried about how they look, and they may be convinced that their bodies, or particular parts of their bodies, are repulsive. For instance, a person with BDD may become obsessed with the size of his or her ears, or may focus on the quality of his or her skin. Because of this obsession the person may spend hours trying to disguise the perceived defect. In severe cases, someone with BDD will become completely convinced that cosmetic surgery in necessary to remove or correct the perceived defect. As might be expected, BDD causes sufferers great anguish, and it is associated with depression, obsessive-compulsive disorder, and eating disorders.

The causes of BDD are not certain, but it is thought that there is a genetic predisposition to the illness, which may be triggered by the changes that take place during puberty. Some research indicates that BDD may also be triggered by chemical imbalances in the brain. Social pressure to look a certain way may contribute to the illness as well. Treatment for this severe distortion of body image usually involves antidepressant drugs and cognitive-behavioral therapy, through which an attempt is made to "retrain" a person's thinking about his or her body. Many doctors are not familiar with the illness, however, and it often goes undiagnosed. Also, many sufferers do not ask for help with their illness, and they are more likely to request surgical procedures that they feel they need.

TOWARD POSITIVE IMAGES OF REAL BODIES

It is only since food became plentiful for the majority in the developed world that thinness has become desirable in Western society. Wallis Simpson, the American-born heiress who became the duchess of Windsor, is often credited with proclaiming in the 1930s that "one can never be too thin or too rich." She was echoing an upper-class obsession with slimness that became prevalent in the twentieth century. Until then, being heavy was a sign that someone was rich enough to have enough to eat, rather than being a part of the "starving masses." In the developing world, and in societies where people are not bombarded by Western media images, thinness is not considered desirable and plumpness is often celebrated. For instance, on the South Pacific island of Tonga, obesity is regarded as a sign of wealth and social status.

Medical experts agree that the media's obsession with thin and unrealistically toned bodies has done more than simply influence people's ideas about body image; it has, in fact, dictated to them which body shapes and weights are desirable. Organizations that promote a healthy, more positive body image urge the media, and particularly the advertising industry, to promote more realistic and normal images. In recent years a few advertisers have consciously reinforced positive images of normal-size women by using "ordinary people" to sell cosmetics, toiletries, and clothes. Nevertheless, the images that surround young people today are still full of thin, unrealistic, and often surgically enhanced bodies.

FURTHER READING

Books

Cash, Thomas F. *The Body Image Workbook: An 8-Step Program for Learning to Like Your Looks.* Oakland, CA: New Harbinger, 1997.

Kirberger, Kimberly. *No Body's Perfect: Stories by Teens about Body Image, Self-Acceptance, and the Search for Identity.* New York: Scholastic, 2003.

Web sites

About.com: Body Image.

From the "About Weight Loss" site, the site contains several links to articles on body image. http://weightloss.about.com/od/bodyimage

GirlsHealth.gov: Body Image and Eating Disorders.

A page designed for younger women, with links to further information on eating disorders. http://www.girlshealth.gov/mind/bodyimage.htm

HealthyPlace.com: Adonis Complex—A Body Image Problem Facing Men and Boys.

Information on the issue of male body image, especially concerning exercise and bodybuilding. http://www.healthyplace.com/Communities/Eating_Disorders/men_1.asp

Media Awareness Network: Beauty and Body Image in the Media.

A site about the media and its influence, designed for teachers, parents, and young adults. http://www.mediaawareness.ca/english/issues/stereotyping/women_and_girls/women_beauty.cfm

SEE ALSO

Anorexia Nervosa; Bulimia; Diet Fads; Obesity; Self-esteem and Food; Weight Loss.

Body Mass Index

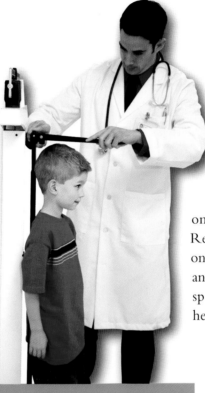

Determining if a person is over-weight is not as easy as looking at a scale. A scale measures how much a person weighs, but it does not indicate whether this is a healthy weight for that person. In the 1980s researchers developed a new gauge, the body mass index (BMI), to help evaluate body weight.

CALCULATING BMI

BMI evaluates a person's weight in comparison with his or her height. The original BMI formula uses metric units: kilograms (kg) for weight and meters (m) for height. The formula is: $BMI = kg/m^2$. The formula for pounds and inches is a bit more complicated: $BMI = lb/in.^2 \times 703$. Either formula should give a number between 19 and 30.

An easier way to figure out BMI is to use a chart or

BMI FOR CHILDREN AND TEENS

Because normal growth rates can vary widely from child to child, BMIs in young people are evaluated in terms of percentiles. A BMI of:

- Less than 5th percentile is considered underweight
- 5th to less than 85th percentile is considered healthy weight
- 85th to less than 95th percentile is considered at risk of overweight
- 95th percentile or greater is considered overweight

online calculator (see Further Reading). BMI charts list height on one axis, weight on the other, and the BMI number that corresponds to each combination of height and weight.

INTERPRETING BMI

For adults, BMI is divided into several weight categories: a BMI of 18.5 or less is classified as "underweight"; the "normal" weight category ranges between 18.5 and 24.9; a person with a BMI between 25 and 29.9 is classified as "overweight"; adults who have a BMI between 30 and 39.9 are classified as "obese"; and a BMI of 40 or greater is considered "extremely obese." A BMI above 25 indicates that someone has too much body fat and a greater chance of developing a long-term illness. Adults whose BMI falls in the normal weight range, 18.5 to

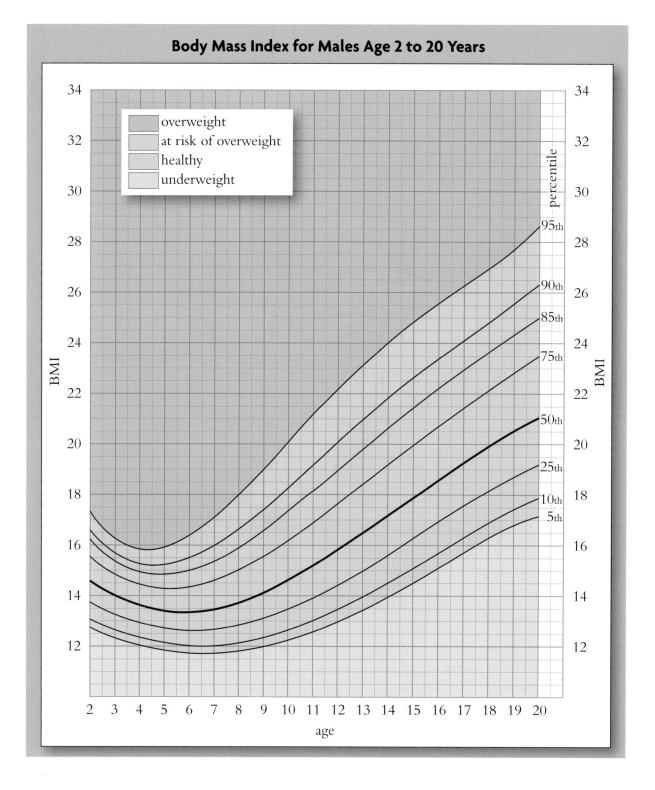

Body Mass Index for Males Age 2 to 20 Years

overweight
at risk of overweight
healthy
underweight

percentile

95th
90th
85th
75th
50th
25th
10th
5th

BMI

age

24.9, are less likely to develop diseases such as heart disease and diabetes.

BMI is evaluated differently for teenagers and children. For these age groups, an individual's BMI is compared with the BMIs of a large group of young people of the same age and gender. BMIs are discussed in terms of percentiles. For example, if a teenager's BMI matches the BMI for the 5th percentile, 5 percent of teenagers of the same age and gender have a lower BMI and

Body Mass Index for Females Age 2 to 20 Years

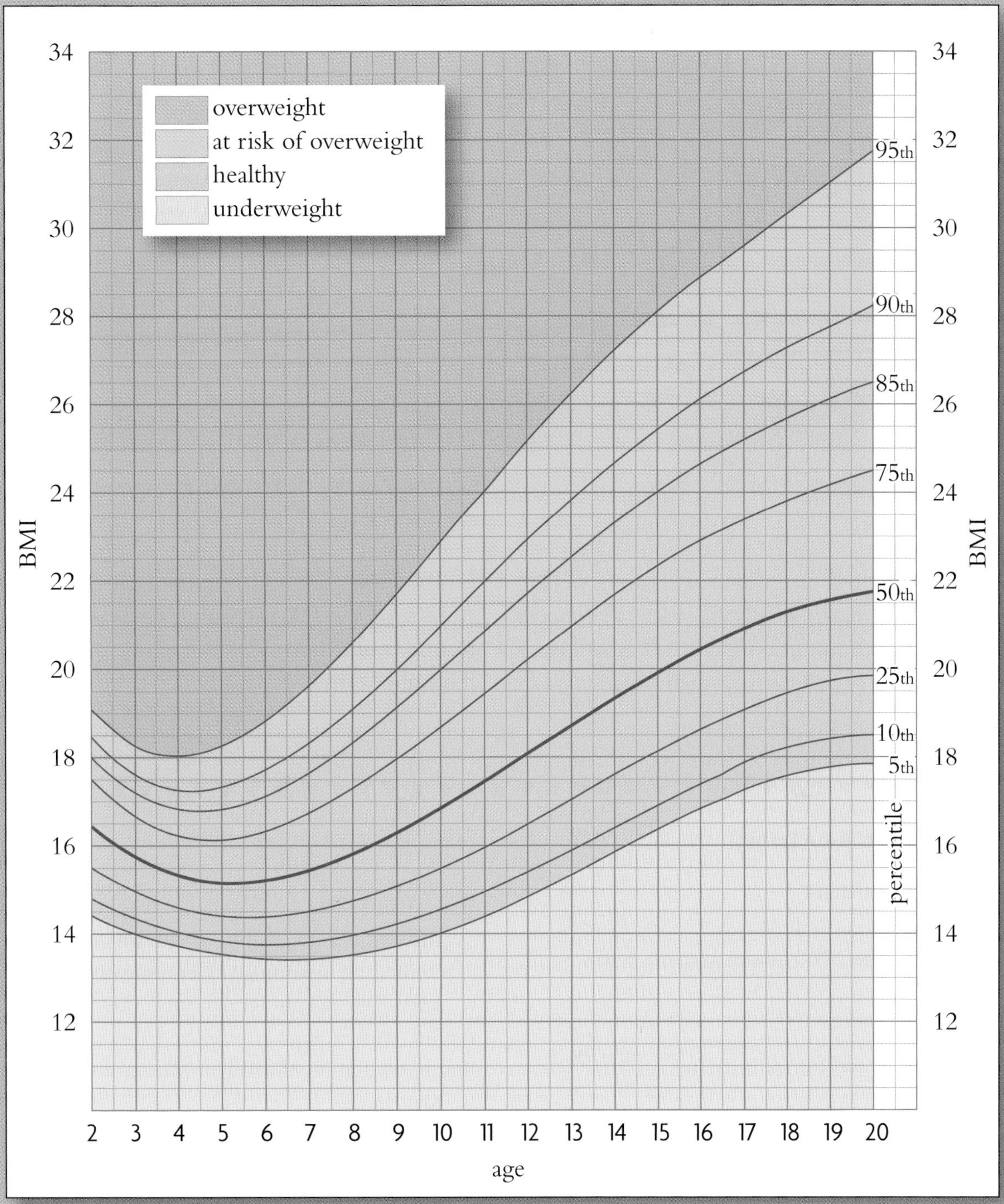
overweight
at risk of overweight
healthy
underweight
34
32
30
28
26
24
22
20
18
16
14
12
BMI
95th
90th
85th
75th
50th
25th
10th
5th
percentile
2 3 4 5 6 7 8 9 10 11 12 13 14 15 16 17 18 19 20
age

95 percent have a higher BMI. A person with a BMI between the 85th and 95th percentiles is considered "at risk" of becoming overweight. A person with a BMI above the 95th percentile is classified as "overweight."

Teenagers who are very muscular and athletic can weigh a lot for their height because muscle is dense and heavy. Such individuals may seem to be overweight or obese according to their BMIs, even though they do not have a lot of body fat.

Because athletes have more muscle mass, which is heavier than fat, their BMIs may classify them as overweight.

A doctor can help determine whether a person needs to lose or gain weight in order to bring his or her BMI into the healthy range. Weight loss, if needed, should be achieved through a combination of a sensible diet and increased physical activity. Achieving and maintaining a healthy weight is one important way to enjoy good health throughout life.

FURTHER READING

Books and articles

Ferrera, Linda A. *Body Mass Index: New Research.* Hauppauge, NY: Nova Biomedical, 2005.

Web sites

Centers for Disease Control and Prevention: Body Mass Index.
This Web site provides information and calculators for both adult and child/teen BMIs.
http://www.cdc.gov/nccdphp/dnpa/bmi
KidsHealth.
The nonprofit Nemours Foundation offers a Web site with health information written for kids and teenagers.
http://kidshealth.org/teen/food_fitness/ dieting/weight_height.html

National Heart, Lung, and Blood Institute: Aim for a Healthy Weight.
The NHLBI's Obesity Education Initiative offers a BMI calculator and charts, along with other methods of measuring risk of being overweight.
www.nhlbi.nih.gov/health/public/heart/obesity/ lose_wt/risk.htm
Partnership for Healthy Weight Management: Body Mass Index.
A BMI chart and calculator, from a coalition of weight loss companies and government agencies.
www.consumer.gov/weightloss/bmi.htm

SEE ALSO

Diabetes; Heart Disease; Obesity; Overweight; Weight Loss.

Botulism

Botulism is a food-borne illness caused by a type of bacteria found in soil. *Clostridium botulinum* (*C. botulinum*) causes nerve paralysis and can be deadly when eaten. It forms spores that remain dormant until growing conditions are ideal—in canned food, for example. As they grow and proliferate, the bacteria spores release botulism toxin, which causes severe illness if ingested. In fact, the U.S. government has classified *C. botulinum* as a potential biological weapon that might be used in a terrorist attack.

There are several types of botulism. People who consume the toxin through already contaminated food contract food-borne botulism. Babies

GUIDELINES FOR SAFE HOME CANNING

- Choose high-quality foods.
- Use a hot-pack method for heating the food before canning.
- Wash jars and lids with hot, soapy water; rinse well.
- Place food into jars according to recipe directions.
- Process the jars in a canner.
- Store for no more than one year.

are especially vulnerable to a particular type of botulism, called infant botulism. Infants have an immature immune system and can become ill from eating foods such as honey, which can contain botulism spores that grow and release toxins once they are in the intestine. A third type of botulism infection, which develops in wounds, is extremely rare.

C. botulinum grows best in low-acid foods in an anaerobic (air-free) environment. Home-canned asparagus, beets, beans, and corn are typical suspects for botulism contamination because they are not acidic, the canning process creates an air-free environment, and home sterilization may not heat the

BOTULISM AND BEAUTY

In 1987 an ophthalmologist in Canada injected a patient with botulism toxin to treat a rare eye disorder that caused frequent blinking. The patient reported back to the doctor that the injections were also taking away her wrinkles. Injections of *C. botulinum*, sold under the name Botox, have since become a popular treatment for wrinkles, because nerves that are paralyzed cannot cause muscles to contract and wrinkle the skin.

release gases that put pressure on the inside of a can or jar; any cans or jars that are bulging or that spurt out their contents when opened should be thrown out. Home-canned, low-acid vegetables and meats should be avoided, unless it is certain that they were canned and heat-treated properly. High temperatures of 240°F to 250°F (116°C to 120°C) in a pressure canner kill the bacteria and destroy the toxin, but spores may not be completely destroyed. The Web sites of the U.S. Department of Agriculture and its county extension offices offer information on safe home canning.

vegetables to a high enough temperature to destroy *C. botulinum*.

SYMPTOMS OF BOTULISM

Botulism affects the nervous system, causing double or blurred vision, drooping eyelids, slurred speech, difficulty swallowing, and weak muscles. In severe cases, a person's arms and legs and the muscles used for breathing become paralyzed, often leading to death.

Symptoms usually develop 18 to 36 hours after the contaminated food is eaten. Doctors diagnose botulism on the basis of a patient's symptoms and brain and nerve testing. In addition, some labs can test for botulism toxin in the affected person's blood or stool.

TREATMENT AND PREVENTION

People who become paralyzed from botulism need intense medical care and may need to be placed on a ventilator. After several weeks, the paralysis may start to subside. An antitoxin that prevents the toxin from causing illness is effective in some less severe cases.

Caution is the best prevention against botulism. Although commercial food manufacturers undergo inspections of their manufacturing processes to ensure that they are following food safety regulations, infection with botulism does occasionally happen. As they grow and reproduce, *C. botulinum* bacteria

FURTHER READING

Rosaler, Maxine. *Botulism*. New York: Rosen, 2004.
Satin, Morton. *Food Alert!: The Ultimate Sourcebook for Food Safety*. New York: Checkmark, 1999.

Web sites
Centers for Disease Control and Prevention: Botulism.
This government agency describes botulism and its symptoms as part of its pages on diseases caused by bacteria.
http://www.cdc.gov/ncidod/dbmd/diseaseinfo/botulism_g.htm
National Center for Home Food Preservation: USDA Complete Guide to Home Canning.
This publication includes instructions for canning several different types of foods.
http://www.uga.edu/nchfp/publications/publications_usda.html
National Institute of Allergy and Infectious Diseases: Botulism.
An overview from this division of the National Institutes of Health and U.S. Department of Health and Human Services.
http://www3.niaid.nih.gov/healthscience/healthtopics/botulism/index.htm

SEE ALSO

Food-borne Illness; Salmonella.

Bovine Growth Hormone

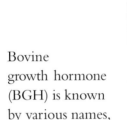

Bovine growth hormone (BGH) is known by various names, including recombinant bovine growth hormone (rBGH), bovine somatotropin (BST), and recombinant bovine soma-totropin (rBST). All refer to the same substance: a genetically engineered version of a hormone that is found in a cow's pituitary gland. (The acronym rBGH is the most common and will be used here.) In its naturally occurring form, the hormone is necessary for the cow's growth, and it stimulates milk production during and after pregnancy. The genetically engineered version of the hormone has been used to

RECORD-BREAKING COW

Two years after rBGH was approved for commercial use, a cow treated with rBGH set a world record, producing 7,737 gallons (29,288 l) of milk in one year. According to an official from the Holstein Association, a cattle industry group, "There was never a cow [producing] over 60,000 pounds before [rBGH] and now we have had four in a year and half."

increase milk production in cows anywhere from 5 to 30 percent.

Since 1993, when it was approved for use in the United States, rBGH has caused controversy. It is the first widespread biotechnology to gain a foothold in the U.S. food supply. As of 2006, approximately one-third of the dairy cows in the United States were being injected with rBGH every 14 days. The hormone supplement is sold under the name Posilac, and the sole producer in the United States is Monsanto, one of the world's leading manufacturers of genetically modified seeds, insecticides, and herbicides.

Bovine Growth Hormone Production

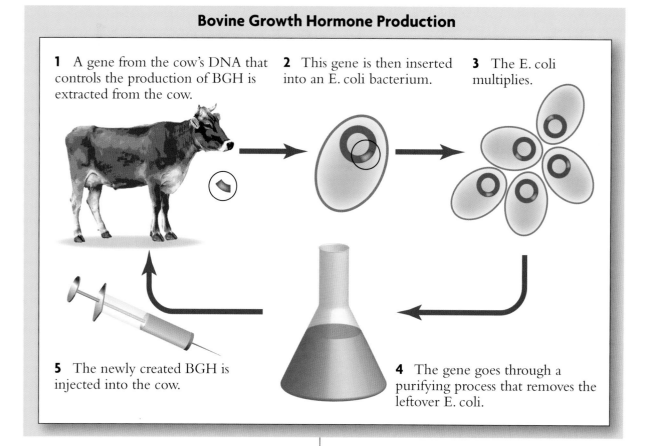

1 A gene from the cow's DNA that controls the production of BGH is extracted from the cow.

2 This gene is then inserted into an E. coli bacterium.

3 The E. coli multiplies.

5 The newly created BGH is injected into the cow.

4 The gene goes through a purifying process that removes the leftover E. coli.

HISTORY

The hormone's potential for stimulating milk production was first discovered by a Russian scientist in the 1930s. Research languished for decades because of low supply (the hormone could be extracted only from slaughtered cows). In the 1970s, however, advances in genetic engineering allowed scientists at the University of California to developed a synthetic version.

Several companies saw the financial potential of rBGH and petitioned the U.S. Food and Drug Administration (FDA) for approval of its use, which was granted in November 1993. By February 1994, rBGH was available for commercial use, and debates about its effect on cows, humans, and the entire dairy industry had already begun.

ARGUMENTS FOR AND AGAINST

Those who support the use of rBGH argue that the hormone is natural and safe, that increased milk production helps feed the hungry, and that higher production will make the U.S. dairy industry more competitive. Those opposed to the use of rBGH are primarily concerned with the effects on animal and human health, and on the survival of small dairy farmers. Of all the concerns, the health effects have elicited the most debate, and each side has scientific studies to back up its claims.

The FDA has long stood by its assertion that rBGH milk is no less safe than "normal" milk. In 1990 a study by two FDA scientists asserted that no adverse health effects were found in rats that had ingested rBGH over a 90-day period. The study, which was commissioned by Monsanto, was the primary basis for the FDA's approval three years later. Since then, a number of studies have confirmed the good health of dairy cows treated with rBGH. Studies on humans have been less conclusive.

Opponents of rBGH cite studies that suggest, but do not prove, that rBGH milk is linked to premature puberty, certain types of cancer, diabetes, and fertility problems in humans. The hormone itself does not directly affect humans. However, the production of another hormone—insulin-like growth factor (IGF-1)—is stimulated by rBGH. Some studies suggest that the levels of IGF-1 are too low to cause significant health effects in humans, but others suggest that IGF-1 can seriously affect the health and fertility of men, women, and children. Again, the research is still inconclusive.

A second issue is the use of antibiotics. Cows treated with rBGH often develop mastitis (an inflammation of the udder) and other health problems that are treated with antibiotics. Some public health experts are concerned that these antibiotics may aid in the development of antibiotic-resistant bacteria, which could create a public health crisis.

GOING ORGANIC

After the initial furor caused by the FDA approval subsided, concerns about rBGH returned to the headlines in the late 1990s, when Canada was grappling with its own approval process. Notably, Canadian scientists looked at the same 90-day rat study that prompted the FDA to approve rBGH in the United States, but they came to a radically different conclusion. They found that rats had absorbed rBGH into their bloodstream and suffered from a weakened immune system. For these and other reasons, Canada denied approval for rBGH in 1999. Allegations that the FDA ignored or suppressed evidence of rBGH's negative health effects prompted two senators from Vermont to request a review of the FDA approval of rBGH.

Meanwhile, activists opposed to genetically modified (GM) food, consumer groups, and small dairy farmers continued to demand that rBGH be banned. Some consumers joined in as well, making their feelings known at the supermarket. In 2005 a study found that the growth in sales of organic milk, which is rBGH-free by definition, was driven by the continued use of rBGH in conventional dairies. This increase in organic milk sales has made it profitable for dairies to become rBGH-free. In 2005 four major dairies in the state of Oregon pledged to keep some or all of their dairy products rBGH-free. In 2006 large dairy farms in Montana and New Jersey followed suit.

MONSANTO FIGHTS BACK

Another way that dairy farmers and consumers have fought against rBGH is with labeling. Currently,

A Wisconsin dairy farmer, pictured with the syringes used to inject rBGH into his cows.

Packaging for Ben & Jerry's ice cream after a lawsuit over the wording of the labels on its rBGH-free products was settled.

there is no way to test milk for rBGH. In order to differentiate themselves from rBGH-users, dairies began to label their products as "hormone-free." Monsanto protested such labeling, arguing that it was false because all milk, technically, contains hormones. The FDA has sided with Monsanto in many instances, warning milk producers against using such labels. With some companies, such as the ice-cream maker Ben & Jerry's, Monsanto has struck a compromise: the company's "no-synthetic hormones" label also acknowledges that rBGH is FDA-approved.

Monsanto has also expanded in other ways, such as exploring the potential of using rBGH in farmed tilapia (a type of fish). In 2006 the FDA approved Monsanto's request to manufacture Posilac entirely in the United States (a key element of the hormone was previously produced in Austria). The change is expected to boost production substantially.

Thirty countries, including Mexico, Brazil, South Africa, India, and Malaysia, have approved the use of rBGH. The National Institutes of Health, the U.S. Department of Health and Human Services, and the World Health Organization have sided with the FDA and the notion that, as milk producers like to put it, "milk is milk." Meanwhile, the European Union, Japan, Canada, Australia, and New Zealand have banned rBGH because of concerns about animal safety and public health.

FURTHER READING

Books and articles

Corey, Beverly. "Bovine Growth Hormone: Harmless for Humans." *FDA Consumer,* April 1990. Available from http://www.fda.gov/bbs/topics/CONSUMER/CON00068.html.

Lyman, Francesca. "What Is in Your Milk?" MSNBC.com, March 29, 2001. Available from http://www.organicconsumers.org/rbgh/msnbconrbgh.cfm.

Web sites

Health Canada: Recombinant Bovine Somatotropin (rbST).
Links to a Health Canada review of rBGH.
   http://www.hc-sc.gc.ca/dhp-mps/vet/issues-enjeux/rbst-stbr/index_e.html

Monsanto: Posilac.
Monsanto's Posilac Web page.
   http://www.monsantodairy.com

University of Minnesota Extension: Dairy Research and Bovine Somatotropin.
A primer on rBGH, with visual aids.
   http://www.extension.umn.edu/distribution/livestocksystems/DI6337.html

U.S. Food and Drug Administration Center for Veterinary Medicine: Bovine Somatotropin.
Links to FDA literature on rBGH.
   http://www.fda.gov/cvm/bst.htm

Vermont Public Interest Research Group: rBGH, Monsanto, and the FDA.
VPIRG's take on the health effects of rGBH. Vermont was one of the first states to initiate rGBH labeling, before the FDA banned its use.
   http://www.vpirg.org/campaigns/geneticEngineering/rBGHintro.php

SEE ALSO

Antibiotics in Foods; Farming, Industrial; Farming, Organic; Genetically Modified Food; Milk.

Bovine Spongiform Encephalopathy

Bovine spongiform encephalopathy (BSE) is an infectious and fatal brain disease of cattle. It is commonly called "mad cow disease" because affected cattle deteriorate both mentally and physically. Since there is no cure for BSE, and no vaccine or treatment to prevent it, animals with BSE need to be slaughtered.

It is believed that eating BSE-infected meat can cause variant Creutzfeldt-Jakob disease (vCJD), a rare but fatal brain disease in humans. For this reason, it is very important that cattle are regularly tested for BSE, and that contaminated meat is prevented from getting into food products for human consumption.

RECOMMENDATIONS

To control BSE, the Food and Agriculture Organization of the United Nations advises the following:

- Use no animal meat or bone products in animal feed.
- Avoid cross-contamination in mills where feed is made.
- Implement safer rendering practices and use very high temperatures.
- Practice active surveillance methods such as checks and lab tests.
- Ban the use of mechanically removed meat.

CAUSES AND SYMPTOMS

Like scrapies, a disease in sheep, BSE is an infectious disease of the brain. Although cattle do not develop scrapies, BSE can apparently develop when they eat food infected with it.

The exact causes of BSE are not fully understood, although researchers know it results from the spread of a misshapen prion, which is a kind of protein normally found in mammals. The misshapen prions cause a "spongelike" appearance to develop in the brain. Other tissues are also infected, including the spinal cord, the intestines, and the entire nervous system. An infected animal will eventually

In 1997 a butcher in London, England, informs customers that beef on the bone has been banned because of concerns about BSE. The ban was a precautionary measure inspired by fears that the marrow inside the bones could transmit BSE.

BOVINE SPONGIFORUM ENCEPHALOPATHY IN THE UNITED STATES

The first case of BSE identified in the United States by the U.S. Department of Agriculture (USDA) was in the state of Washington, in December 2003, in a cow that had been brought from Canada. The animal's meat had been used in food products that, as much as possible, were recalled. There have been very few identified cases in the United States since then, partly because of strict import controls.

A second potentially infected cow was identified in November 2004. In June 2005, after running additional tests in conjunction with a laboratory in the United Kingdom, the USDA confirmed that the cow had, indeed, tested positive for BSE. However, the meat from that cow had never entered the food supply.

develop symptoms such as nervousness or aggressiveness, and it will start to stagger. Cattle then usually die within weeks, if they are not slaughtered first.

The spread of BSE is thought to have been fostered by animal feeding practices that had been particularly common in Europe and other parts of the world in the years after World War II. Cattle were given feed that contained processed animal products created by "rendering," a process in which animal matter is boiled at a high temperature to remove water and separate fat, after which the remaining substance is ground up. During the 1970s, the rendering process changed and a lower temperature was used. It is suspected that this change in feeding practices contributed to the spread of BSE in the 1980s.

The disease has an incubation period of four to seven years, so the symptoms were not immediately obvious until hundreds of thousands of cattle had been infected. In the 1980s and 1990s, many farms in Great Britain and elsewhere in Europe were forced to slaughter their stock as an epidemic took hold and governments imposed

COOKED BEEF

Meat from animals with BSE cannot be used for food because the infected prions that cause the disease easily survive normal cooking temperatures.

strict measures to try to eradicate BSE. British beef exports to European countries were banned from March 1996 until March 2006; this ban was very damaging to the British beef industry. Although the first case of BSE was identified in Great Britain in 1986, some experts believe that BSE emerged spontaneously, and it was just bad luck that the first case happened to be found in Great Britain. However, other experts point to the fact that Great Britain is unusual in having a higher proportion of sheep than cows, and sheep offal (leftover parts of butchered animals) was commonly put into animal feed, a practice that not all countries followed.

CONTROL

In most developed countries, government regulations have been imposed in an effort to prevent the spread of BSE. However, some countries, particularly in eastern Europe, have less than rigorous surveillance. Many countries have imposed strict import and export controls to prevent contamination from animals with BSE and to prevent the importation of meat

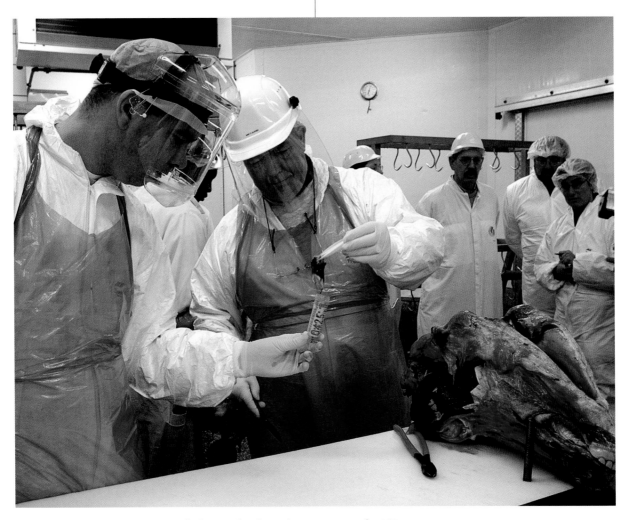

Dutch scientists take a tissue sample from a slaughtered cow to test it for BSE.

products from countries that do not follow strict regulations.

In March 2006, scientists in Texas succeeded in cloning a goat fetus that lacked prions, the type of protein that is infected by BSE. It is hoped that without prions, animals could be safe from BSE. Although there is no cure or vaccine for BSE, researchers believe that one way to eradicate the disease may be to use similar techniques to produce genetically modified cattle that are immune to BSE.

FURTHER READING

Books and articles

Ferreiro, Carmen. *Mad Cow Disease (Bovine Spongiform Encephalopathy)*. Philadelphia, PA: Chelsea House, 2005.

Sheen, Barbara. *Mad Cow Disease*. San Diego, CA: Lucent, 2005.

Web sites

World Health Organization: Bovine Spongiform Encephalopathy.
A detailed fact sheet about BSE.
http://www.who.int/mediacentre/factsheets/fs113/en/

United Kingdom Department of Environmental, Food, and Rural Affairs: Bovine Spongiform Encephalopathy.
The BSE Web site offered by DEFRA provides detailed information, FAQs, a glossary, and links to other sites.
http://www.defra.gov.uk/animalh/bse/index.html

U.S. Department of Agriculture: Bovine Spongiform Encephalopathy (BSE) Resources.
A fact sheet with links to many other resources on BSE, from the USDA.
http://www.fsis.usda.gov/Fact_Sheets/Bovine_Spongiform_Encephalopathy_BSE/

SEE ALSO

Beef; Farming, Industrial; Food and Drug Administration.

Branding

Brands are names, logos, symbols, or features that distinguish one product from other similar products. For the food industry, in which supermarket freezers may hold more than a dozen types of vanilla ice cream and the shelves may hold a number of identically shaped bags of sugar, branding is important for consumers and manufacturers alike. For consumers, brands help clarify the differences among the overwhelming number of products available. Consumers learn to trust individual brands, and they develop expectations about and associations with a product or its manufacturer. For example, some brands are thought of as "high-quality" brands, some are considered "low-cost," and others come to be known as "healthy." For food manufacturers, branding is one of the most powerful tools used to sell products, not just once, but over and over again.

Brands themselves consist of little more than icons or logos. These deceptively simple images are meant to convey much larger values and ideas, which are communicated to the public through advertising and marketing. These larger ideas create a strong relationship between a consumer and a product. This relationship, or "brand loyalty," is the holy grail of food manufacturing.

THE EARLY DAYS OF BRANDING

The idea of brands is centuries old. In the thirteenth century, for example, King John of England ordered bakers to mark their loaves of bread. These marks

(RE)BRANDING THE TOOTHFISH

Sometimes, foods need a little help from branding experts. In the late 1970s, the Patagonian toothfish was rechristened as the Chilean sea bass, although it is not a bass and does not necessarily come from Chile. Under its new name, the Patagonian toothfish is served in restaurants and sold at a premium in stores. The same fish is known as *merluza negra* in South American countries, where it is a fairly cheap fish, and as *mero* in Japan, where it tends to be expensive. Illegal overfishing in various parts of the world threatens the future of the species.

Manufacturers hope to use branding to persuade customers to choose their product over similar, competing products.

helped buyers of that era to identify the wares of different bakers. Once they had tasted and decided which qualities they preferred—whether it be a saltier, crusty loaf or a sweeter, chewier one—people could seek out the same baker's bread in the future. The consumer could trust that he or she would get the same product each time, and the producer could trust that the customer would return.

When the methods of the industrial revolution were applied to food production in the nineteenth century, branding became even more important. Sugar manufacturers, meat packers, cereal makers, and other makers of widely distributed food products began to use advertising to promote their distinct brands. With the advent of new communications technologies, such as radio and television, advertising drove branding to new heights. Brands that once relied on taste, price, quality, or convenience to attract customers began, through marketing, to create more complex associations involving social status, achievement, or lifestyle.

MODERN BRANDS

For decades, Coca-Cola has been one of the most recognizable brands in the world. The simple logo—Coca-Cola written in a distinctive white cursive type against a red background—adorns cans, glass and plastic bottles, and other paraphernalia. From the earliest days, Coca-Cola used advertising to make lifestyle associations with its brand. An ad from 1907 reads: "Coca-Cola is full of vim, vigor, and go," thus associating Coke with energy and excitement. In 1971 Coca-Cola famously portrayed a type

of global friendliness, with its "I'd like to buy the world a Coke" campaign. To this day, the company spends millions of dollars to spread awareness of the Coca-Cola brand. Other top food brands include the fast-food chain McDonalds, Coca-Cola's competitor Pepsi, and the cereal maker Kellogg's.

Food production in the twenty-first century is a global industry generating more than $3 trillion a year, and the branding of food has likewise flourished. For example, Pizza Hut was named the most trusted food brand in India in 2006, for the fourth year in a row.

As different groups of people seek out new and different features in their food, food branding is changing. The surge of organic food products now available has been, in part, a result of successful branding, marketing, and advertising. Foods branded "organic" have been linked in the minds of many with powerful terms such as "natural" and "healthy." Nonetheless, these products are manufactured, and so they are therefore not entirely "natural." Indeed, they may be high in sodium or calories or may be otherwise unhealthy.

FURTHER READING

Books and articles
Gobé, Mark. *Emotional Branding: The New Paradigm for Connecting Brands to People.* New York: Allworth, 2001.

Web sites
Forbes: Brand Values.
An interactive site that explores various products and brands.
   http://www.forbes.com/technology/
   2005/06/01/05bbsbrandsland.html
Interbrand: Best Global Brands 2007.
Businessweek and Interbrand rank top global brands.
   http://www.interbrand.com/best_brands_2007.asp

SEE ALSO

Marketing; Packaging; Processed Food.

Bread

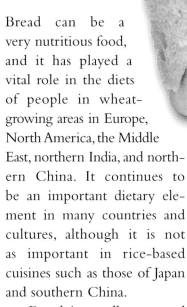

Bread can be a very nutritious food, and it has played a vital role in the diets of people in wheat-growing areas in Europe, North America, the Middle East, northern India, and northern China. It continues to be an important dietary element in many countries and cultures, although it is not as important in rice-based cuisines such as those of Japan and southern China.

Bread is usually prepared by baking dough, which is made from flour, water, and other ingredients. Breads that contain yeast, a living organism that has the effect of "rising" or adding air to dough, are called leavened breads. Those made without yeast are called unleavened breads or flatbreads.

Bread can also be raised by adding bicarbonate of soda (also called baking soda); the resulting loaves are called soda breads.

In broad terms, different basic types of bread can be distinguished by color and by the kind of flour used to make them. The flour will vary according to the type of grain used, and also according to which parts of the grain are retained when the flour is milled. Milling is the process of grinding the wheat grains so that the bran and wheat germ are separated from the inner kernel. This is now often done with automated machinery in large commercial operations, although smaller commercial flour mills were once a common sight in villages and towns throughout the United States,

SOME TYPES OF BREAD

- Bagels
- Baguette
- Banana bread
- Brown bread
- Challah
- Chapati
- Corn bread
- Focaccia
- Naan
- Pita bread
- Pumpernickel bread
- Roti
- Rye bread
- Sourdough bread
- White bread
- Whole wheat bread

The taste, texture, and nutritional value of breads vary widely, depending on how the bread is made. For example, rye bread has less gluten than wheat, which is why rye bread is heavier.

Canada, and Europe. These mills were powered by wind or water, or even by a horse pulling the millstones around as part of "the daily grind." Before that, humans did the work, as they continue to do in many parts of the developing world.

Only two types of flour can be made into leavened bread: wheat and rye. These are the only flours that have enough of a particular protein, called gluten, that traps the gases given off by the fermenting yeast, enabling the bread to rise. There are three general types of leavened breads produced with wheat:

- *Whole wheat bread* uses flour made from the whole wheat grain, including the bran and wheat germ. This is the most nutritious

form of flour. In North America, bread cannot be called whole wheat unless it contains whole grain flour.

- *Brown bread* is sometimes made with whole grain flour, but more often it contains caramel coloring to make it look brown.
- *White bread* is made from white flour that has had the wheat germ and bran removed. The white flour may also have been bleached with either potassium bromate or chlorine dioxide to help make it brighter and help improve the way it cooks. In North America, the law says that white flour must be enriched with added vitamins that replace some of those lost by bleaching. White bread is easy to digest but is low in fiber.

Within these broad categories, the types of flour used in bread can vary considerably. For example, the white flour used in making French baguettes is a special kind that produces a distinctive crust.

THE ORIGINS OF BREAD

Although no one is certain exactly how and why bread was first made, its common main ingredient, wheat, has been cultivated since the dawn of civilization. Stone Age people would probably have used hot stones to bake flat cakes made of wheat kernels mixed with water. Later on, the wheat grains would have been sheared or ground and used to make flat bread, very similar to the flat breads sometimes eaten today, such as pita bread and chapati.

There is evidence of both milling and making bread with yeast dating back to at least 1000 BCE in Egypt. From there it came to Greece, and the Romans later spread it across Europe. At medieval feasts a special, very thick bread called trencher bread was used as a plate for meat, but it was probably not eaten itself. There is also a long tradition of ornaments and decorations made from bread dough that is painted and varnished after baking.

There was a time when baking bread was an onerous task, and the necessary fuel was too expensive for all but the rich. In the Middle Ages a baker might bake someone's raw dough in the oven in exchange for a fee, or people would go to the baker's shop daily to buy a loaf to eat that day. In these shops, bread came in different qualities, depending on the type of flour used. In general, the whiter the flour, the more expensive the bread.

Flour can be made from different grains, depending on cultural preferences or the availability of ingredients. Not only wheat, but also oat, rye, and barley flour can be used, as well as more unusual flours, such as chickpea and potato. American settlers initially had no wheat and made bread primarily from cornmeal. They later grew wheat when they settled in regions with a suitable climate. There is still a great tradition of making corn bread in North America, however, particularly in areas where corn is easy to grow.

In 1928, Otto Frederick Rohwedder (1880–1960), from Davenport, Iowa, designed a bread-slicing machine and took it to a baker he knew in Chillicothe, Missouri. The presliced bread sold well, and Rohwedder soon became known as the "father of sliced bread." By the 1930s, the Continental Baking Company had made sliced bread popular across North America with its Wonder Bread brand presliced loaf. About 33 percent of all bread sold at this time was sliced. During World War II, metal was needed for making weapons, so bread slicing was prohibited, and some machines were melted down. Sliced bread was off the menu until it was reintroduced in the 1950s and became extremely popular.

In modern times, bread can be baked at home in the oven, or special bread-baking machines that automate the process and save time can be used. Even so, most people choose to buy their bread at a baker or supermarket, since bread is one of the easiest and least expensive foods to obtain. There are also a great variety of breads available from these sources.

BREAD AND CIRCUSES: THE POLITICS OF BREAD

In the first century CE the Roman emperors provided unlimited free wheat (for making bread) to the poor, and they also sponsored chariot racing, or "circus games." They did both in order to keep the populace happy and less likely to rise up in protest against their poverty. The Roman poet Juvenal coined the phrase *panem et circenses* (bread and circuses) to mock this practice. In modern times, the phrase "bread and circuses" is used to criticize any government policy that tries to keep people superficially happy with cheap entertainment or food while failing to address fundamental needs such as education, democracy, or human rights.

MAKING BREAD

Bread is usually made by baking. The basic ingredients in yeast-based bread are flour, liquid, and yeast. Salt and a small amount of sugar (or honey or molasses) can also be added; both help to preserve the bread and add flavor. Bread recipes vary, but the yeast is often first mixed with sugar and liquid (often water or milk) and left for a few minutes. This allows the yeast to start the fermentation process that is essential for introducing carbon dioxide bubbles into the dough, improving the texture and making the bread rise. The yeast mixture is gradually added into the flour, and the bread is kneaded for a few minutes, either by hand or in a food processor (or, in commercial bakeries, in large machines).

Flour contains two proteins—glutein and gliadin—which combine with water to form gluten. When dough is kneaded, the gluten gradually becomes more elastic, and strands of stretched gluten can be seen in the dough's texture. The gluten helps to form the pockets of carbon dioxide gas produced by the yeast. The dough is then left to rise, during which time the yeast continues to grow and the dough expands. It is then shaped or placed in a loaf pan and left to rise for an additional (but shorter) time. All this has to be done before baking begins; once the bread is in the oven, the yeast is killed by the high temperature and the gluten hardens, so no further rising can take place. Flour that has only a small amount of gluten compared with wheat, such as rye flour, produces loaves that are denser and do not rise a great deal.

Another way of raising bread is by using a starter dough, which is a homegrown yeast mixture made from flour and water. Placed in a container and left in a warm place, this mixture will eventually grow yeast, which will continue to grow if fed with additional flour and water. Some of the starter dough is used in place of the yeast in bread such as sourdough bread.

Some people are allergic to gluten and need to avoid eating bread unless it is made with special gluten-free flour, which is often made from milled

A bread factory in Mexico City. Mass-produced, uniformly shaped bread originated in England but is now common in many parts of the world.

TYPE OF BREAD	SERVING SIZE	ENERGY (kcal)	PROTEIN (g)	TOTAL FAT (g)	DIETARY FIBER (g)	CARBOHYDRATES (g)	CALCIUM (mg)
Bagels	1 bagel (71 g)	182	7.11	1.15	1.6	35.86	63
Banana bread	1 slice (60 g)	196	2.58	6.30	0.7	32.76	13
Corn bread	1 piece (60 g)	188	4.32	6.00	1.4	28.86	44
Italian bread	1 slice (30 g)	81	2.64	1.05	0.8	15.00	23
Mixed grain bread	1 slice (26 g)	65	2.60	0.99	1.7	12.06	24
Pita bread	1 piece (60 g)	165	5.46	0.72	1.3	33.42	52
Pumpernickel bread	1 slice (26 g)	65	2.26	0.81	1.7	12.35	18
Rye bread	1 slice (32 g)	83	2.72	1.06	1.9	15.46	23
Sourdough bread	1 slice (32 g)	92	3.76	0.59	0.8	18.06	14
White bread	1 slice (25 g)	66	1.91	0.82	0.6	12.65	38
Whole wheat bread	1 slice (28 g)	69	3.63	0.94	1.9	11.56	30

Notes: Bagel (plain, onion, poppy, or sesame, enriched, with calcium propionate); banana bread (prepared from recipe, made with margarine); corn bread (prepared from dry mix); mixed grain bread (includes whole grain and seven-grain); pita bread (white, unenriched).

Source: U.S. Department of Agriculture, Agricultural Research Service, USDA Nutrient Data Laboratory. USDA National Nutrient Database for Standard Reference, Release 19. 2006. Available from http://www.ars.usda.gov/nutrientdata.

rice. In this case, the bread is usually raised with bicarbonate of soda, which produces carbon dioxide bubbles through a different process.

BREAD IN DIFFERENT CULTURES

Historically, bread has often been used as a symbol for food and sharing in many cultures—to "break bread" together is to share a meal. Indeed, bread is so important in the human diet that it is used in some religions to symbolize life or God. In Christianity, for example, Christ's body is represented by the bread given to worshippers during a Communion service. In Islam, bread is referred to as God's blessing.

The fact that so many types of bread exist shows just how integral bread is to different cultures and countries. For example, Indian cuisine has many different types of unleavened flat bread, such as naan, chapati, and roti. Served with a meal, these

In 2005 at Xiakou Village, in the Qinghai province of northwest China, a woman piles up an offering of bread for the gods during the Nadun Festival.

Bread dough must be kneaded repeatedly in order to stretch out the gluten.

breads are often stuffed with chopped vegetables and meat and used to scoop up food. In Italy, a wide range of breads are eaten, including focaccia, which is similar to pizza dough and is flavored with olive oil and herbs. Breads originating from traditional Jewish culture include challah, a rich yeast bread containing eggs and sugar, and bagels, which are cooked by boiling and then baking. Handcrafted traditional breads of any kind, made by a skilled baker, are sometimes referred to as artisanal breads.

BREAD AND NUTRITION

Bread is a source of calcium in the diet and also provides iron, some B vitamins, folic acid, selenium, and dietary fiber. Bread is also rich in complex carbohydrates. These are carbohydrates that contain both starch and fiber, so that they need to be broken down by digestion before the body can use them as energy. Complex carbohydrates are more beneficial than simple carbohydrates.

Some low-carbohydrate diets encourage people to give up eating bread and characterize bread as a fattening food. However, this need not be the case if bread is eaten as part of a normal, balanced diet, particularly if it is a whole-grain bread. Nutritionists and medical professionals generally agree that bread is a valuable and enjoyable source of a wide range of important nutrients.

FURTHER READING

Books and articles

Duff, Gail. *Bread: 150 Traditional Recipes from around the World*. New York: Maxwell Macmillan International, 1993.

Ingram, Christine, and Jennie Shapter. *The World Encyclopedia of Bread and Bread Making*. New York: Lorenz, 1999.

Web sites

Botham and Sons Bakery: The Story behind a Loaf of Bread.
Information about the history of bread and how it is made.
http://www.botham.co.uk/bread

Odlum Group: The Story of Milling.
A Web site that shows all the stages involved in getting wheat from the field, through the commercial milling process, and into the stores as flour.
http://www.odlums.ie/pages/milling.htm

The Science of Cooking: Bread.
A page with activities and bread recipes, and information on what happens during the baking process.
http://www.exploratorium.edu/cooking/bread/index.html

SEE ALSO

Baking; Fiber, Dietary; Grains; Religion and Food; Sandwich; Wheat; Whole Grains; Yeast.

Breakfast

Breakfast is the first meal of the day, eaten soon after waking. The word *breakfast* comes from the notion of breaking the fast that occurs as a result of being asleep for several hours. There are many different traditional breakfast dishes across the world. However, eggs, breads, and hot drinks (especially coffee and tea) appear in a great many breakfast meals.

Nutritionists and medical researchers agree that skipping breakfast can be detrimental to health, resulting in difficulties in concentration and possibly long-term effects on the metabolism (the body's ability to turn food into energy). Studies have shown that people who eat a nutritious breakfast are more likely to obtain the vitamins and minerals the body needs, have lower levels of cholesterol, and be generally more energetic. Despite this, many people choose not to eat breakfast, either because of a lack of time or because of a mistaken belief that this will help them to lose weight (see Box, Missing Out). Concern over the trend away from eating breakfast has led the United States and many other countries to provide school-age children with a nutritious breakfast at school, through school breakfast programs and other similar plans.

MISSING OUT

In 2006 a study by researchers in Houston, Texas, discovered that of 700 ninth graders, nearly 20 percent did not eat breakfast. These children were less likely to obtain the recommended intakes of calcium, iron, and a wide variety of other nutrients.

The same year, another study in Massachusetts showed that students who began to eat breakfast regularly increased their scores in math and English tests by up to 3 percent.

In the later nineteenth century, breakfast cereals became particularly popular in the United States, in part as a result of the efforts of religious groups like Seventh-Day Adventists, who believed in eating a vegetarian diet. In the twentieth century, the American breakfast incorporated a variety of convenience foods, often frozen (such as frozen waffles) or purchased from fast-food outlets on the way to work or school (such as muffins and doughnuts).

BREAKFASTS AROUND THE WORLD

The influence of U.S. culture on the rest of the world is such that people in many Westernized

A kindergartner eats breakfast at his desk in Harrisburg, Pennsylvania. School breakfast programs provide many students with nutritious meals.

HISTORY OF BREAKFAST

In Britain from the fifteenth through the seventeenth centuries, it was common for farm laborers to eat only a light meal of bread and a hot drink for breakfast. The main meal, called dinner, was eaten in the late morning, after several hours of work in the fields. This practice gradually began to change, and by the nineteenth century, breakfast had become a more elaborate cooked meal—especially among members of the upper class, who had the leisure time to sit for an extended meal and often had no need to work. The typical contemporary American cooked breakfast has its roots in English Victorian traditions, but it has also incorporated "native" foods such as corn and grits (coarsely ground wheat or corn, cooked in water), and immigrant foods, such as bagels (from Jewish cuisine) and doughnuts (possibly brought by Dutch settlers).

Croissants are sometimes served as part of breakfast in France.

Breakfast, Szechwan-style, with steamed buns and spicy noodles.

countries also eat American-style convenience foods for breakfast. However, many different traditional breakfast foods are still eaten widely. In Europe the "continental breakfast" usually consists of coffee, either black or with milk, served with breads and pastries. In England the traditional "full English breakfast" of cooked eggs with sausage ("bangers"), bacon ("rashers"), and fried or steamed vegetables is eaten less often than cereals and toast. In Germany, Switzerland, and other parts of northern Europe, cold meats, hard-boiled eggs, and yogurt are common breakfast foods.

Asian breakfast foods vary significantly from country to country, and even from region to region. It is not unusual to eat savory pickled meats or fish, or rice dishes, as well as steamed sweet buns and cakes. In the Middle East, beans and meat dishes are often served.

In the United States, breakfast at home often consists of cereal, coffee or milk, and bread or toast. There are many variations, however, such as waffles and syrup or a pork roll with grits. Brunch, a meal that is midway between a breakfast and lunch, has also become a popular meal, especially on weekends.

FURTHER READING

Books and articles

Calhoun, Richard S. *Breakfast around the World.* Williamsport, PA: Peach Blossom, 2002.

Culinary Institute of America. *Culinary Institute of America: Breakfast and Brunches.* New York: Lebhar-Friedman, 2005.

Figtree, Dale. *Eat Smarter: The Smarter Choice for Healthier Kids.* El Monte, CA: ZHealth, 2006.

Hagen, Brenda Ann, and Weber State University School of Education. *Universal School Breakfast.* Ogden, UT: Weber State University, 2006.

Schaefer, Lola M., and Schaefer, Ted. *Breakfast.* Oxford, U.K.: Raintree, 2006.

Web sites

KidsHealth: Ready, Set, Breakfast!

An article for kids that explains why eating breakfast is so important to good health.
http://www.kidshealth.org/kid/stay_healthy/food/breakfast.html

Mayo Clinic: Healthy Breakfast—The Best Way to Begin Your Day.

An article that explains how eating a good breakfast benefits health.
http://www.mayoclinic.com/health/food-and-nutrition/NU00197

Mr. Breakfast: International Breakfast Recipes.

A resource with many different recipes from around the world.
http://www.mrbreakfast.com/category.asp?categoryid=3

Recipe America: Breakfast Recipes.

A list of typically American breakfast recipes.
http://www.recipeamerica.com/recipes/breakfast.htm

SEE ALSO

Cereals; Diet, Balanced; Dinner; Eggs; Lunch; Meals.

British Cuisine

Between 1850 and 1930, the British had one of the world's most influential cuisines, with British chefs introducing and disseminating new ideas about cooking and new ways of processing food. Although jokes about the poor quality of British food are common, British cuisine provided the basis of the foods of the United States, Canada, Australia, and New Zealand, and it had a major influence in many other parts of the world.

HISTORY

Until the nineteenth century, the cuisine of Great Britain (England, Wales, Scotland, and Northern Ireland) had been

MRS. BEETON

In the 1850s, Isabella Beeton began publishing installments of her *Book of Household Management*. It was to include 100 recipes for soup, 200 for sauces, and similar numbers for other dishes, as well as hints on how to run a house. It was one of the most successful cookbooks ever published and was taken to every part of the British Empire. A revised version of "Mrs. Beeton" has remained in print, even as it has been succeeded by other British cookbooks by authors such as Delia Smith and Nigella Lawson.

typical of northern Europe. The small upper class ate a diet that was essentially a cousin to French cuisine, based on meats, white flour, white sugar, and butter. Everyone else survived on soups and dark breads. In the nineteenth century, however, this sharp division began to disappear. As an ever-increasing part of the British population acquired the right to vote, they also demanded the right to eat meat and white bread. In 1846 Parliament repealed the laws that had put high taxes on imported wheat; as a result, the price of wheat bread fell. A small island, Britain increasingly relied on imported food to feed its growing population. Wheat came from Russia, India, Canada,

Great Britain

Shetland Islands

Orkney Islands

Outer Hebrides

North Sea

SCOTLAND

NORTH ATLANTIC OCEAN

Edinburgh

NORTHERN IRELAND

Belfast

Isle of Man

Dublin

IRELAND

ENGLAND

WALES

Cardiff

London

St. George's Channel

English Channel

FRANCE

☆ national capital

Yorkshire Pudding

Yorkshire pudding is a savory dish related to the American popover. Named for the county called Yorkshire, the pudding accompanies roast beef.

1 pint (500 ml) milk
1 ⅓ cups (335 ml) flour
3 eggs
1 pinch salt
Dripping (melted fat) from roast beef or spray oil (easier but less authentic)

About half an hour before the beef has finished roasting at 400°F (200°C), take out a muffin pan designed to make eight muffins. Pour a little fat from the roasting beef into each indentation, or use can of spray oil to coat each one. Heat in the oven for five minutes. Put flour, eggs, milk, and salt in a bowl and beat with a balloon whisk until combined. Pour into the molds. Place in the oven and bake for 25 to 30 minutes. They will puff magnificently. Remove Yorkshire puddings and beef from the oven. Place the puddings around the beef while you make the gravy. Give each person one pudding with slices of beef and gravy.

and the United States; beef came from Argentina; lamb and mutton came from Australia and New Zealand; sugar came from the Caribbean; bacon came from Denmark; and tea came from China and India.

The industrialization of food processing and cooking further reduced the price of food, making what had been luxury items for the rich available to the whole population by the early twentieth century. Huge roller mills replaced water mills for grinding flour, and refineries for sugar were established in port cities. Factories turned out crackers, cookies, jams, margarine, pickles, candies, and condiments such as curry powder and Worcestershire sauce. Running water, gas ovens, and, later, electric stoves were installed in home kitchens. Urban housewives began shopping in grocery stores pioneered by entrepreneurs such as Thomas Lipton (now best known for tea).

Between 1850 and 1950, housewives in the new urban middle class, many of whom had never had to cook complicated dishes before, faced high expectations. Their family meals were supposed to be an occasion for family unity, for teaching children how to be good citizens, and for supplying good nutrition. This task became increasingly complicated during a period in which scientists discovered proteins, carbohydrates, and vitamins. For help in achieving these goals, housewives turned to a growing number of cookbooks and magazines.

BRITISH DISHES

From the eighteenth century on, Great Britain's signature dish was roast beef, the traditional Sunday midday dinner. As beef was still an expensive luxury, pork and lamb roasts were also popular. Roasts were accompanied by white bread, potatoes, and gravy. Gravy is a sauce based on a roux, a combination of fat from the roast and white flour, to which stock or water is added.

Spices were used sparingly in main dishes, though many sauces and dressings included fresh herbs, such as mint, parsley, and sage. Hot mustard, pepper, and horseradish provided spiciness. An increasing number of bottled condiments were available, many of them inspired by the cuisines of Britain's overseas colonies. The fish sauces of Southeast Asia were transformed into Worcestershire sauce or ketchup, which was made with mushrooms or nuts before it became tomato-based in the late nineteenth century. The curries of India were the basis for curry powder, which the British exported worldwide. Cakes, puddings, pastry, and sweet biscuits (cookies) were also based on white flour and fat (usually butter or margarine), with the addition of eggs, rising agents, and flavorings such as orange or lemon, cinnamon, nutmeg, and allspice.

Tea, which the British began drinking in quantity in the nineteenth century, accompanied both breakfast and the meal called "tea." A full English breakfast, eaten at nine in the morning after a couple of hours of work, consisted of three courses: oatmeal; a savory course such as scrambled eggs, eggs and bacon, or smoked fish; and then toast and orange marmalade. Tea was served

buffet-style some time between four and six. Homemade savory sandwiches, sweet sandwiches, small cakes, and large cakes were eaten, in that order, accompanied by tea. For the upper classes, tea was a light snack to bridge the gap between lunch and a late dinner. For the middle and working classes, it was the last meal of the day. High tea—with canned cold meats and, for special occasions, a dessert such as jelly (similiar to Jell-O)—was the emblematic working-class meal.

Prior to the 1960s, Britain did not have a restaurant cuisine. The wealthy preferred to eat in private houses or private clubs; the middle class thriftily ate at home; and the working class, without facilities to cook at home until well into the twentieth century, bought take-out foods such as fish and chips (french fries). The scarcity and poor quality of the few restaurants contributed to the dismal image of British cooking in the eyes of visiting foreigners.

The British exported food-processing methods such as canning, industrialized brewing, and industrialized baking, as well as many foodstuffs, such as crackers, to all parts of the British Empire, which at its height in the 1930s directly ruled about a quarter of the habitable surface of the globe (and indirectly controlled much more). Millions of Britons emigrated to the United States, Canada, Australia, and New Zealand, taking with them their entire cuisine. These two factors,

The kitchen at Café Lazeez, a chain of Indian restaurants that opened in Britain in the early 1990s.

It is not uncommon for people with bulimia to keep their binge eating a secret from loved ones.

diagnosed, and their true number is hard to ascertain; some researchers estimate that more than two million adolescent girls in the United States may have bulimia.

CAUSES OF BULIMIA

People with bulimia have obsessions with food and with body weight—they are constantly preoccupied with food and eating, and they frequently have very low self-esteem. Whereas people with anorexia nervosa eat too little, people with bulimia eat too much (although it is not unusual for someone to suffer from each condition in turn). Because of the purging behavior that follows binge eating, people with bulimia are not necessarily obese, or even overweight—indeed, people with bulimia can be any weight. However, the behavior can result in severe health problems; bulimia has also been associated with an increased risk of depression and suicide.

The practice of binge eating and purging is certainly not new, but only in modern times have possible causes begun to be more fully investigated. Current research indicates that bulimia is a psychiatric disorder, which can be triggered by a variety of genetic and environmental factors. Research has shown that people with severe bulimia may have abnormalities in the chemicals in their brain, and that the illness tends to run in families. Other research indicates that there is also a connection between bulimia and depression and other psychiatric conditions, such as obsessive-compulsive disorder (OCD). Some studies have pointed toward the influence of social factors, such as the effect of parental criticism during childhood or the modern cultural obsession with thinness.

Scientists and the medical profession agree that there is no single cause of bulimia, and that it can occur with different degrees of intensity. The onset of bulimia most commonly occurs during the teenage years, when self-consciousness about appearance may be at a particularly high level. It is important that people with bulimia are diagnosed as early as possible, because without treatment the disorder can continue for many years.

should somehow control through willpower. The modern medical profession recognizes that this is not the case, however, and the American Psychiatric Association formally recognized bulimia as a disorder in 1980. It is one of three recognized eating disorders, along with anorexia nervosa and binge eating; in the latter, people binge-eat but typically do not purge.

Although the majority of people diagnosed with bulimia are white, the condition is not restricted by race. In the twenty-first century, in fact, increasing numbers of women of color are struggling with bulimia. Also, statistics from the U.S. National Institute of Mental Health indicate that between 5 and 15 percent of people with anorexia nervosa or bulimia are male. People with bulimia will often eat secretly, and even close family members may not be fully aware of their illness. Because of this, many bulimics are not

HEALTH ISSUES AND RISKS OF BULIMIA

Bulimic binge eating and purging can give rise to a number of severe health problems, some of which can be life-threatening:

- As a result of vomiting, tooth enamel can be eroded by long-term exposure to stomach acid.
- Vomiting can also result in nutritional deficiencies, and vital minerals, such as potassium, can be lost. This loss causes metabolic disturbances, contributes to lowered resistance to infection, and can lead to fatal heart failure.
- Other effects of bulimia can include muscle spasms, impaired mental activity, and organ damage (for example, the stomach can split open).
- Vigorous exercise may cause dehydration or long-term bone loss (through calcium deficiency).

- In women and girls, menstruation may stop or become irregular.
- People with bulimia often also struggle with addictions to drugs or alcohol.
- Bulimics may suffer from clinical depression or other depressive anxiety disorders.
- There is a high incidence of suicide among people with bulimia.

HOW BULIMIA IS TREATED

Therapies for bulimia are based on the fact that it is a psychological illness and that recovery involves acknowledging the underlying emotional issues and making lifestyle changes. Psychotherapy is an important aspect of treatment for bulimia, since it can offer help in addressing problems of low self-esteem, depression, and obsession with food and body image.

Nutritionally, many people with bulimia have no sense of what "normal" eating is, so they need help in relearning a healthy approach to food and eating. A registered dietitian may assist in supply-

The Council of Fashion Designers of America (CFDA) Health Initiative held meetings in 2007 to address eating disorders in the fashion industry.

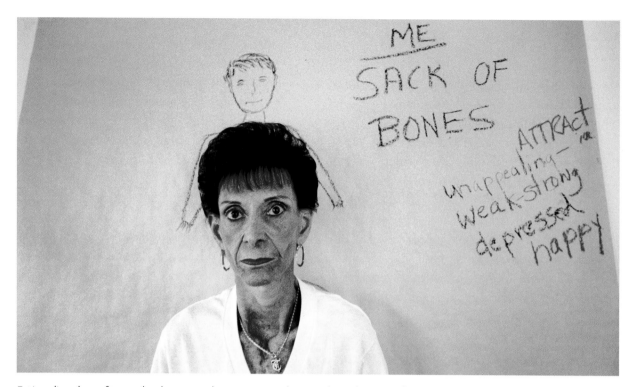

Eating disorders often strike the young, but many people struggle with eating disorders throughout their lives. This patient at the Renfrew Center in Florida poses with her art therapy project in 2006.

ing menus and information on balanced foods and nutritional requirements. Similarly, medical treatment with antidepressant drugs can help to alleviate feelings of anxiety and underlying depression, with some patients being treated in a hospital or specialized center. There are several organizations to assist those with bulimia in finding the best treatment options.

FURTHER READING

Books and articles

Claude-Pierre, Peggy. *The Secret Language of Eating Disorders: How You Can Understand and Work to Cure Anorexia and Bulimia.* New York: Vintage, 1998.

Greenfield, Lauren. *Thin.* San Francisco: Chronicle, 2006.

Hall, Lindsey, and Leigh Cohn. *Bulimia: A Guide to Recovery.* 5th ed. Carlsbad, CA: Gürze, 1999.

Hornbacher, Marya. *Wasted: A Memoir of Anorexia and Bulimia.* New York: Harper Perennial, 1999.

Web sites

National Eating Disorders Association.

Information on eating disorders and how to find treatment.

http://www.nationaleatingdisorders.org

TeensHealth: Eating Disorders—Anorexia and Bulimia.

Friendly information designed for a teen audience.

http://kidshealth.org/teen/your_mind/ mental_health/eat_disorder.html

SEE ALSO

Anorexia Nervosa; Body Image; Obesity; Overeating; Overweight; Self-esteem and Food; Weight Loss.

Butter

Butter is a highly concentrated form of the fat found in milk. Historically, butter has been considered a luxury food, in part because it is labor-intensive to produce. Used as a spread, butter adds a rich flavor to foods like bread, toast, or pancakes. It also plays a crucial role in cooking: it can be used to fry foods or serve as the basis of sauces. When used in baking, it helps to bind ingredients together.

Butter is most commonly made from the milk of cows, but it can also be made from the milk of sheep, goats, horses, and some other mammals. It is made by churning soured milk or cream until the fats separate from the liquid (buttermilk), leaving a semisolid substance. People have probably known how to make butter since pre-

historic times. In fact, the world's peoples have long been separated into those who eat butter and those who do not. Sometimes considered a sacred substance, butter plays a role in traditional ceremonies in many cultures.

BUTTER-MAKING TECHNOLOGIES

Until around 1850, butter was produced in the United States exclusively on farms, by people using churns. One popular type of churn used well into the twentieth century was essentially a tall canister fitted with a paddle. Archeological evidence suggests that as early as 3500 BCE the people of Sumer, in Mesopotamia (modern-day Iraq), shook cream in a vertical churn that was strikingly similar in shape. In contemporary times, butter is

THE BUTTER-STINKERS

As people who consumed little animal fat and virtually no dairy products, the Japanese were very sensitive to the strong body odor of Westerners they encountered in the nineteenth century. The Japanese blamed butter for the stench, and they called Westerners *bata-kusai*, or "butter-stinkers." The phrase *bata-kusai* is still used to describe things that are offensively Western. Butter has been part of the Japanese diet since the 1960s, although per capita consumption is only about one-third of what it is in the United States.

A typical butter churn for home use.

Modern commercial butter production reflects two important technological advances. One, the mechanical cream separator, was introduced in the United States around 1880. The machine uses centrifugal force to separate the cream from milk. By the mid-twentieth century, another machine, the high-speed continuous churn, had been commercialized. Sweet, uncultured cream is pasteurized and pumped into one end of the machine, and butter and buttermilk come out the other end. During the final stage of continuous churning, water is beaten into the butter. In addition, salt, beta-carotene (a pigmented compound used for adding color), and preservatives are often used as well. Butter in the United States is rated AA, A, or B, according to government standards for flavor, consistency, color, and salt characteristics.

NUTRITION

Most commercial butters contain at least 80 to 82 percent milk fat, and some dairies produce richer butters containing up to 86 percent milk fat. Water (around 16 percent) and milk solids (1 to 1.5 percent) make up the rest of butter. A small amount of salt is often added as a preservative, but unsalted butter is also available.

still occasionally churned by hand (indeed, making butter at home as a kitchen experiment can be fun), but most butter is produced by machines.

Butter is high in calories—about 100 per tablespoon (14 grams). It is an excellent source of

BUTTER: NUTRITION INFORMATION							
TYPE OF FOOD	SERVING SIZE	ENERGY (kcal)	PROTEIN (g)	TOTAL FAT (g)	SUGARS (g)	SODIUM (mg)	CALCIUM (mg)
Butter, unsalted	1 tbsp (14.2 g)	102	0.12	11.52	0.01	2	3
Butter, salted	1 tbsp (14.2 g)	102	0.12	11.52	0.01	82	3
Margarine	1 tbsp (14.2 g)	101	0.13	11.35	0.00	133	4
Whipped butter	1 tbsp (9.4 g)	67	0.08	7.62	0.01	78	2

Notes: Margarine (industrial, soy, and partially-hydrogenated soy oil, use for baking, sauces and candy); whipped butter (with salt).

Source: U.S. Department of Agriculture, Agricultural Research Service, USDA Nutrient Data Laboratory. USDA National Nutrient Database for Standard Reference, Release 19. 2006. Available from http://www.ars.usda.gov/nutrientdata.

vitamin A, which is needed for maintaining good vision. Butter contains all the other fat-soluble vitamins (D, E, and K), and a number of trace minerals, including selenium, a powerful antioxidant. Butter also contains several valuable fatty acids: butyric acid is used in the colon as an energy source; lauric acid combats bacterial and fungal infections; and conjugated lineolic acid (CLA) boosts the immune system. Like other animal-derived fats, butter is high in cholesterol and saturated fats, which, if consumed in excessive amounts, can cause hardening of the arteries and contribute to heart disease.

COMMON TYPES OF BUTTER

Several varieties of butter are widely available and are suited to specific uses:

Light (also called reduced-calorie or "lite") butter contains 50 percent less fat than regular butter and has higher water content. Useful as a spread, it is not appropriate for cooking or baking.

Whipped butter is produced by injecting nitrogen gas into butter as it is whipped. It spreads very easily, even when cold, but is not appropriate for cooking.

Cultured butter is made from cream that has been slightly fermented through the addition of lactic acid. It has a faint sour taste and odor.

Clarified butter is made by melting unsalted butter over low heat, simmering it for about 15 minutes, then skimming off the milk solids. The resulting clear, yellow liquid will not burn when used to pan-fry foods, and it keeps about three times longer than traditional butter.

Ghee is a form of clarified butter that is cooked longer, so that the sugars in the butter are caramelized. A staple in the cuisine of India, it has a distinctive nutty flavor and will keep for up to two months in a cool cupboard.

BUTTER LORE WORLDWIDE

In ancient times, butter was used not just for food. It was also used as fuel for lamps, in religious rituals, and as a coating to protect the skin from cold and

MARGARINE

Margarine is the best known of various butter substitutes made from vegetable oils (sometimes in combination with nondairy, animal-based fats) rather than milk fat. Margarine was invented in France in 1869, during the Franco-Prussian War. In the face of butter shortages, Emperor Napoléon III organized a competition to produce a cheaper substitute. The winner, Mège Mouriès, mixed oil from beef fat with skimmed milk, water, and a strip of a cow's udder to produce an early type of imitation butter. However, it was inferior in flavor and was white, not yellow, in color.

Since that time, butter substitutes have improved considerably. Modern margarines are commonly made from different vegetable oils, such as soy, cottonseed, palm, canola, peanut, coconut, safflower, or sunflower oils. Often beta-carotene is added as a coloring agent.

Vegetable oils do not naturally harden when chilled, as dairy fat does. Therefore, to make margarine more like butter in consistency, the oils are hydrogenated—treated with hydrogen, in the presence of nickel—to harden them. Soft margarine is not treated in this way, and it is often high in polyunsaturated fats, which are healthier than saturated fats.

Formerly, margarine was touted as being healthier than butter, but this has since been disproved. Both butter and hard margarine are high in saturated fats, and they have the same amount of calories. Further, the process of hydrogenation used to make hard margarine produces trans fatty acids (TFAs, or trans fats). Transfats have been shown to raise levels of "bad" cholesterol in the bloodstream even more than saturated fats do.

insects. Over time, different "butter cultures" emerged in different regions. In Hindu mythology, ghee is said to have been created by Prajápati, the Lord of Creatures, who then poured it into fire to create his children. The pouring of ghee into fire became a ritual that reenacted this creation myth.

A Tibetan monk makes a flower out of yak butter in 2007.

Smen (also *semneh* or *samneh*) is a traditional Middle Eastern cooking oil created by clarifying butter made from sheep or goat milk and adding herbs and spices. Similar to ghee but sharper in fragrance and flavor, it is a prized flavoring ingredient and represents the riches of the household.

Yak butter is a central part of the diet in Tibet. It is consumed in salty butter tea, a warming drink greatly appreciated in the cold climate. The staple Tibetan dish is *tsampa,* made from salted tea, yak butter, and barley pounded together. Yak butter is also used in lamps, and for centuries Tibetans celebrated a Festival of the Butter Gods, for which Buddhist monks spent months carving huge sculptures of gods and mythical subjects out of butter.

Maslyanitsa is the Russian word both for butter and for the festival that marks the end of winter and welcomes summer. Orthodox Christians celebrate this Butter Week just before giving up butter for Lent. People eat blini, or pancakes, with honey, caviar, fresh cream, and butter. The more abundant the butter, the hotter the sun is supposed to be in the coming summer.

In contemporary Western culture, butter is appreciated more for its flavor and its culinary properties than for its symbolic importance. As in ancient times and across cultures, however, it is a valued substance that many people consider a treat.

FURTHER READING

Books and articles

McGee, Harold. *On Food and Cooking: The Science and Lore of the Kitchen.* New York: Scribner, 2004.

Web sites

Web Exhibits: Butter.
A very detailed virtual exhibit on the history of butter and butter making, with "how-to" links to topics such as making butter and ghee at home.
http://www.webexhibits.org/butter

SEE ALSO

Antioxidants; Cholesterol; Cooking Oils and Fats; Fatty Acids; Saturated Fats; Vitamins, Fat-soluble.

Caffeine

Caffeine is a natural stimulant that speeds up responses in the brain and nervous system, leading to other physiological changes in the body, particularly an increase in heart rate. In addition to affecting the body, it is also psychoactive—that is, it changes one's mood.

Foods that are naturally high in caffeine include coffee, tea, and chocolate. Caffeine is also added to many other products, including soft drinks and energy drinks. Although caffeine can reduce fatigue and make a person feel more alert and energetic, it is also addictive and can have side effects that pose health risks. On the other hand, low doses of caffeine have been found to be beneficial in some circumstances.

SOURCES AND HISTORY

The most commonly consumed source of caffeine is the coffee plant, first grown in Ethiopia, from which caffeine gets its name. Caffeine is also found in the tea leaf, the cacao pod, and the kola nut. The cacao plant, a small evergreen tree related to the cola tree but from tropical Mexico, is the source of cacao beans, used to make both cocoa powder and chocolate. The kola nut is the fruit of a group of 125 species of trees in the genus *Cola*, which are native to tropical Africa and Indonesia. The bitter brown seed is the source of cola extract, originally used in cola drinks but subsequently replaced by synthetic ingredients. Both cacao and cola plants are now cultivated widely in tropical regions as food crops. Other plants with high levels of caffeine include the ilex plant, originally from Brazil and used in a popular South American tea called yerba maté (YER-ba MA-tay), and the cassina tree, found in parts of North America.

CAFFEINE LEVELS

Approximate caffeine levels in a six-ounce (170 g) cup of various drinks:

- Black tea: 70 mg
- Brewed coffee: 120 mg
- Colas and caffeinated soft drinks: 45 mg or more
- Energy drinks: 80 to 200 mg
- Green tea: 35 mg
- Instant coffee: 80 mg

Calcium deficiency can be prevented by taking supplements. People taking supplements should take two or three small doses (500 to 600 mg) per day, rather than one large dose. Taking the supplements with meals increases the amount of calcium that is absorbed.

FOOD SOURCES OF CALCIUM

Many people already know that milk and other dairy products are high in calcium, but the mineral is also found in a wide variety of other foods, including leafy green vegetables, nuts, seeds, tofu, and dried fruit (see box, Calcium in Foods). In the United States, Canada, and some European countries, commercially produced white flour is fortified with calcium. Meat and fish are not especially rich sources, because most calcium in animals is stored in the bones (and therefore not eaten). Canned fish, if eaten with the bones, is a notable exception. Dairy products are a good source of calcium in a form that is easy for the body to absorb. The calcium in foods that contain oxalic acid, such as spinach and chard, is more difficult for the body to

Industrial Uses

Calcium is used in the production of cements and in making calcium alloys. For example, lead-calcium alloys are used in making large storage batteries. Their many uses include power for large equipment, trains, and ships.

ABOVE: Natural calcium deposit in Pamukkale, Turkey.

and strength. Within the body, calcium is continually being shifted from the skeleton to the blood, where it is used in body processes, before being reabsorbed into the bones. This absorption is called bone mineralization and is regulated by hormones, especially vitamin D (technically not a vitamin but a prohormone, or hormone precursor).

The amount of calcium required each day varies, depending on age and gender, and it can even vary within individuals. This is partly because the body adapts to calcium intake and absorbs less calcium when the amount coming into the body increases. In addition, other minerals work in conjunction with calcium within the body. Excess calcium is eliminated from the body in urine, feces (bowel movements), and sweat. The rest is stored as part of bone mineralization.

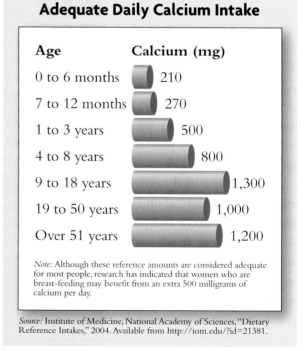

Adequate Daily Calcium Intake

Age	Calcium (mg)
0 to 6 months	210
7 to 12 months	270
1 to 3 years	500
4 to 8 years	800
9 to 18 years	1,300
19 to 50 years	1,000
Over 51 years	1,200

Note: Although these reference amounts are considered adequate for most people, research has indicated that women who are breast-feeding may benefit from an extra 500 milligrams of calcium per day.

Source: Institute of Medicine, National Academy of Sciences, "Dietary Reference Intakes," 2004. Available from http://iom.edu/?id=21381.

SELECTED FOOD SOURCES OF CALCIUM

FOOD	CALCIUM (mg)	PERCENT DAILY VALUE
Yogurt, plain, low-fat, 8 oz. (250 ml)	415	42
Yogurt, fruit, low-fat, 8 oz. (250 ml)	245 to 384	25 to 38
Sardines, canned in oil, with bones, 3 oz. (90 ml)	324	32
Cheddar cheese, 1 ½ oz. shredded (45 ml)	306	31
Milk, nonfat, 8 oz. (250 ml)	302	30
Milk, whole, 8 oz. (250 ml)	291	29
Mozzarella, part skim 1 ½ oz. (45 ml)	275	28
Tofu, firm, made with calcium sulfate, ½ cup (125 ml)	204	20
Orange juice, calcium-fortified, 6 oz. (180 ml)	200 to 260	20 to 26
Salmon, pink, canned, solids with bone, 3 oz. (90 ml)	181	18
Pudding, chocolate, instant, made with 2% milk, ½ cup (125 ml)	153	15
Cottage cheese, 1% milk fat, 1 cup unpacked (250 ml)	138	14
Tofu, soft, made with calcium sulfate, ½ cup (125 ml)	138	14
Spinach, cooked, ½ cup (125 ml)	120	12
Frozen yogurt, vanilla, soft-serve, ½ cup (125 ml)	103	10
Ready-to-eat cereal, calcium-fortified, 1 cup (250 ml)	100 to 1,000	10 to 100
Turnip greens, boiled, ½ cup (125 ml)	99	10
Kale, cooked, 1 cup (250 ml)	94	9
Kale, raw, 1 cup (250 ml)	90	9
Ice cream, vanilla, ½ cup (125 ml)	85	8.5
Soy beverage, calcium-fortified, 8 oz. (250 ml)	80 to 500	8 to 50
Chinese cabbage, raw, 1 cup (250 ml)	74	7

Notes: Daily Values (DV) were developed to help consumers determine if a typical serving of a food contains a lot or a little of a specific nutrient. The DV for calcium is based on 1,000 mg per day. Calcium values for tofu are only for tofu processed with a calcium salt. Tofu processed with a non-calcium salt will not contain significant amounts of calcium.

Source: Office of Dietary Supplements, National Institutes of Health. Available from http://dietarysupplements.info.nih.gov/factsheets/calcium.asp.

absorb because the calcium and oxalic acid combine to form calcium oxalate, a chemical salt that the body cannot use as efficiently.

Eating a healthy diet that contains calcium from a selection of foods offers the most benefit. Even though calcium is found in many food sources, some experts estimate that between 50 and 70 percent of adults in the United States eat much less calcium than is recommended, generally owing to a poorly balanced diet.

CALCIUM DEFICIENCY

Without sufficient vitamin D, calcium bone mineralization can be disrupted, and this disruption will affect the structural integrity of the skeleton. Rickets, a childhood disease caused by chronic (long-term) vitamin D deficiency, causes bones to become soft and deformed because of a lack of calcium. Children with this disease develop a bowlegged appearance, as well as other bone deformities. Rickets is rare in

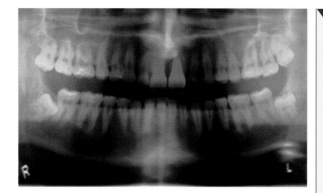

A panoramic X-ray of a mouth. Calcium is a vital component in bones, cartilage, and teeth.

the early twenty-first century, largely due to a program of vitamin D supplements in developing countries and in the United States and Canada a legal requirement to fortify milk with added vitamin D. Cases of rickets have been identified, however, in infants fed rice milk and other unfortified milk substitutes.

Low levels of calcium in the blood can cause a condition called hypocalcemia. Symptoms include muscle spasms, tingling, and numbness. Hypocalcemia is usually caused by a hormonal imbalance rather than diet.

Insufficient calcium in the diet can contribute to osteoporosis, a bone-thinning disease that can start affecting people when they are in their thirties. It is considered a serious health risk to people, especially women, who are over the age of fifty. Although some decrease in bone density is normal as people age, osteoporosis makes bones brittle and more likely to break. Studies indicate that calcium supplementation can be beneficial in delaying the onset of osteoporosis, and it is particularly beneficial to women over thirty. Females with chronic weight loss due to anorexia nervosa have a high risk of developing osteoporosis at an unusually young age.

Calcium alone cannot prevent bone loss, and doctors generally advise a well-balanced diet and weight-bearing exercise in addition. Vitamin D (through food and also exposure to sunshine) is also essential.

FURTHER READING

Books and articles

Bruce, Bonnie and Gene A. Spiller. *Calcium: Nature's Versatile Mineral*. New York: Avery, 2000.

Natow, Alice B. *Calcium Counts*. New York: Pocket Books, 2000.

U.S. Department of Health and Human Services. *Bone Health and Osteoporosis: A Report of the Surgeon General*. Washington, DC: DHHS. Available from http://www.surgeongeneral.gov/library/bonehealth.

Weaver, Connie, and Robert Proulx Heaney. *Calcium in Human Health*. Totawa, NJ: Humana, 2006.

Web sites

National Institute of Child Health and Human Services: Milk Matters for Kids.

Information on calcium with links to further resources including a list of foods that are good sources of calcium.
http://www.nichd.nih.gov/milk/kids/kidsteens.cfm

National Institutes of Health, Office of Dietary Supplements: Dietary Supplement Fact Sheet: Calcium.

Information on recommended levels and calcium's role in health and diet.
http://dietary-supplements.info.nih.gov/factsheets/calcium.asp

National Osteoporosis Foundation.

Statistics, facts, and resources on osteoporosis.
http://www.nof.org

U.S. Food and Drug Administration: Calcium! Do You Get It?

A calcium education program aimed at girls ages 11 to 14, with quizzes, activities, and other teaching tools.
http://www.cfsan.fda.gov/~dms/ca-toc.html

SEE ALSO

Cheese; Iron; Milk; Minerals; Rickets; Sodium; Vitamins, Fat-soluble.

Index

Page numbers in **boldface** type refer to article titles.

Page numbers in *italic* type refer to illustrations or other graphics.

Photo Credits

I know that. I need to get
something before I go back.

Back where?

But Iceland isn't a continent.

What, no smart remarks?

Well, you do sound like you swallowed a computer. But I suppose there are lots of interesting things in the world.

Besides musk oxen?

Possibly. But don't tell anyone I said that.

So, are you ready to go home?

Not yet. I want to visit one more place.

South America

This is South America. It has both the largest tropical rainforest in the world and one of the longest mountain ranges in the world.

H

FOR THE ANCIENT INCAS, LOSING A GAME OF BASKETBALL WAS PARTICULARLY EMBARRASSING — THE LOSERS HAD ALL THEIR CLOTHES TAKEN AWAY.

Cool.

NORTH AMERICA EUROPE SALE

Fine. I'll tell the facts.
Did you know that the Grand
Canyon is one of the world's
largest canyons and that Lake
Superior is one of the world's
largest freshwater lakes?

Wow. That's a
whole lot of large.

Kind of like
your ego.

What did I say
about jokes?

Sorry. Are you ready for the last continent?

But the coolest
part is the Arctic.

If by coolest you
mean coldest.

THE MOKAYA PEOPLE
INVENTED HOT CHOCOLATE
NEARLY 4000 YEARS AGO.
UNFORTUNATELY, THEY
DID NOT INVENT
MARSHMALLOWS.

You should probably let me tell the jokes.

North America

Yay! I like North America. North America has Alaska. That's where I live. And Canada. That's where my aunt lives.

There's more to North America than the Arctic.

I think we'd better go to
North America. Fast.

Finally! Something fun to do!
I'm going sliding on the ice.

Watch out for
those tourists!

Europe has lots of fun things to see:
the Eiffel Tower, Stonehenge, lots of castles.
There's also Eisriesenwelt in Austria.

Eisriesenwelt is the
largest known system
of ice caves in the world.

Did you just scream like a baby?

No.

Then why are you in my arms?

I'm . . . just trying to protect you from all those scary creatures.

Whatever. Let's go to Europe.
Maybe you won't be so afraid there.

Australia is home to the box jellyfish and a type of snake called the inland taipan. Those are some of the world's most venomous creatures.

Eeek!

Welcome to the
Land Down Under.

The land down under what? My feet?

I mean Australia. It's called the
Land Down Under because
it's south of the equator.

Australia

Z.BRA

FRICA

ANTARCTICA

HYSTERICAL
H
MARKER

ACCORDING TO LEGEND,
ULURU ROCK WAS MADE BY TWO
BOYS WHO PLAYED IN THE MUD.
ACTUALLY, IT IS MADE OF
SANDSTONE, WHICH MAKES IT
ONE OF THE BIGGEST
SANDCASTLES EVER

Are there any musk oxen there?

No.

Then why bother going?

Asia is also the biggest continent
and has the most people.

People? You mean those funny looking, two-legged,
hairless things? That's boring. Who wants to
be with a bunch of people?
Let's go somewhere else.

MANY HUMANS CONSIDER
THE OX TO BE SACRED.
THIS MAY BE WHY
MUSK OXEN THINK THEY
ARE SO SPECIAL.

Fine. Let's go to Australia.

Asia has the world's tallest mountain,
Mount Everest, and the world's longest
man-made structure, the Great Wall of China.

This wall could use some
pictures on it. Good thing
I brought some.

Asia

HYSTERICAL
H
MARKER

THE MORTAR THAT HOLDS
TOGETHER THE STONES AND
BRICKS OF THE GREAT WALL
IS MADE OF RICE FLOUR.
SO FAR NO ONE HAS EVER
TRIED TO EAT THROUGH IT.

Wait, you mean there's more?
Which one do we get to see next?

Well, we've been going in
alphabetical order so far,
so let's visit Asia and then
we'll go to Australia.

AFRICA

ANTARCTICA

Do they all start with A?

Antarctica is also the
largest desert in the world.

I thought deserts had to be hot.

Nope, just dry.

SOUTH
POLE

Like your sense of humor?

Very funny. Would you like to
visit another continent?

LAWRENCE
OF
ANTARCTICA

Did you know that
Antarctica is the
windiest continent
on earth?

Really.
I hadn't
noticed.

You know what I just realized? You live in the hottest place on earth and I live in the coldest.

Actually the Arctic isn't the coldest place on earth. Antarctica is.

Who said anything about ants in the Arctic?

Antarctica. It's on the opposite side of the world from the Arctic.

And it's cold? I want to see it.

And I just found
something very good.

Those are wildebeests.
They're also called gnus.

Well, I just want to *call*
them. Hello, ladies!
Is it hot out
here or is it me?

And look at the
savannah with
all its grass.

I like this.
It's not
frozen.

See, there are lots of
good things about Africa.

Here, wear this.

Ahh, that feels good.

Now can you see how amazing Africa is?
See how the desert sands look like waves?

Africa

AFRICA IS HOME TO THE
WORLD'S LARGEST LIVING
LAND ANIMAL, THE AFRICAN
ELEPHANT, WHICH CAN
WEIGH 14,000 POUNDS,
ABOUT THE SAME AS $21\frac{1}{2}$
MUSK OXEN.

HYSTERICAL
H
MARKER

Personally I think
Africa is the best.

Africa? Never
heard of it.

You've never heard of Africa?
That's where I live.

Well, no wonder
I've never heard
of it. Everybody
must be trying
to forget it.

That's it. We're going
to Africa. I'm going
to show you just
how amazing it is.

But it's only
got the Arctic.
The world's a lot
bigger than that.

Now you're talking crazy.
The Arctic has to be the biggest
part because it's the best part.
That's where musk oxen live.

What do you mean?
Nothing happened to it.

the world according to musk ox

erin cabatingan
illustrated by matthew myers